More praise for *Investing in Apartment Buildings*

Matthew's newest book, *Investing in Apartment Buildings*, couldn't have come at a more poignant time in our lives. He offers a modern-day, step-by-step survival guide for the ever-growing economic war on the middle class. Win your own financial war by arming yourself with Matthew's systematic, hands-on experience and sound principles for investing in apartment buildings.
— RYAN ZAHORUIKO, PRINCIPAL, FOREST STREET PROPERTY LLC

Matt Martinez is able to take the complicated world of real estate investing and put it into terminology that the average person is able to understand. Understanding the acquisition of apartment buildings is not an easy task, but Matt makes it clear and concise in his book. He gives the reader the tools, knowledge, and desire; it is only up to the reader to follow what he reads to give him success.
— SETH HELLER, VP OF ACQUISITIONS, GREC CONVERSIONS LTD

Matt Martinez makes a compelling case as to why real estate investing remains the best path to financial independence. *Investing in Apartment Buildings* provides step-by-step advice that gives newcomers to real estate investment the practical advice they need to learn the business from the ground up. The chapter summaries provide an excellent tool to focus the reader, and the real-life "war stories" provide great context for each lesson. If you want to get started in developing an independent income stream, *Investing in Apartment Buildings* should find a place on your bookshelf.
— JORDAN C. PAUL, CEO, AQUILA PROPERTY COMPANY, INC.

I bought my first rental property around 1990. Since that time I've bought, operated, and sold more than 3,000 apartment units, which have generated more than $30MM in net profits. If I had had Matt's book in 1990, I could have avoided dozens of pitfalls and accelerated my growth *much faster*.
— DAVID F. ATKINS, PRESIDENT, ALEXANDER FORREST PROPERTIES

Matthew Martinez has done it again! His books are clear, compelling, and always offer tremendous knowledge and value for anyone wishing to get into the real estate market. Speaking from experience, Matthew provides great insight into real estate investing, and you'll even get to read personal e-mail exchanges from Matthew's treasured mentor.
— PHOEBE CHONGCHUA, REAL ESTATE COLUMNIST

Matt has really hit the target: a concise, complete, and organized approach to investing in this asset class. Apartments, with their short lease terms, are true inflation hedges, and this book can help your investment approach, whether you are new to the business or a seasoned veteran. He really gets it, and you will, too.
— GARY KACHADURIAN, CHAIRMAN, APARTMENT REALTY ADVISORS

A must read for anyone looking to invest in apartment communities. Matt's book is both informative and interesting!
— MARK H. STERN, SENIOR VICE PRESIDENT OF ACQUISITIONS, WATERTON RESIDENTIAL

An outstanding summary of the key principles of real estate investment and wealth accumulation. Matt Martinez has the unique ability to transform sophisticated ideas and concepts into highly readable and entertaining prose. This is required reading for anyone serious about learning the basics of apartment building investment in these complex times.

—RICHARD N. BERNSTEIN, ATTORNEY AND PRINCIPAL SHAREHOLDER, GREENBERG TRAURIG LLP

Because of Martinez's vast understanding of the real estate industry's many nuances, he is able to provide real and sustainable advice for investment professionals and novices alike. Martinez will show you where the rubber meets the road when it comes to multiunit success. Buy this book!

—CHARLES BYRON ANDREWS, FOUNDER, BLUE COAST ASSET MANAGEMENT

This is an outstanding guide for those who are interested in investing in apartment buildings. Matt Martinez has created a well-thought-out and informative book for the novice, intermediate, and experienced multiunit apartment investor. He discusses in great detail farm areas, sourcing properties, value-add deals, property management, value determinations, financial analysis and underwriting guidelines, negotiating strategies, and how to succeed in this challenging but rewarding business. He also uses real-life examples to help the reader better understand the principles he teaches. This is an outstanding book that anyone who is seriously interested in apartment buildings must read!

—ROB SENA, PARTNER, ALTERRA CAPITAL GROUP

When I started in real estate investing, Matt Martinez sat down with me and explained how to do things properly. His guidance gave me both the analytical framework and the courage to succeed. This book encapsulates much of his wisdom and is definitely a must read for anyone serious about real estate investing.

—BEN GOODMAN, FOUNDER, FASTFORWARDS MANAGEMENT LLC

Investing in Apartment Buildings is not only another story of success, but one that lets you profit from Matthew Martinez's experience. The writing style makes you feel like you're talking with a friend. This book provides a great description of the current industry's situation, ideas to capture opportunities, and tools to assess each investment. It represents a very compelling guide to help you ask the right questions and understand the answers when considering real estate deals.

—JAVIER DBORKIN, DIRECTOR, BOSTON ANDES CAPITAL

Any seasoned multifamily investor will tell you that the fortunes you hear about are made and lost in the details. Many of the lessons I have learned through years of trial and error have been clearly laid out in a highly accessible format in Matt Martinez's *Investing in Apartment Buildings*.

—MATT WANDERER, PRINCIPAL, ALTERRA CAPITAL GROUP

Matt's approach to investing in multifamily apartments is concise, strategic, and up-to-date. This book is well thought out and informative for today's multifamily investors. Matt knows what he is talking about. His book is a must read.

—JOEL WEBB, FOUNDER, THECREATIVEINVESTOR.COM

INVESTING IN
APARTMENT
BUILDINGS

CREATE A RELIABLE STREAM OF INCOME
AND BUILD LONG-TERM WEALTH

MATTHEW A. MARTINEZ

New York   Chicago   San Francisco   Lisbon   London
Madrid   Mexico City   Milan   New Delhi
San Juan   Seoul   Singapore
Sydney   Toronto

The *McGraw·Hill* Companies

1 2 3 4 5 6 7 8 9 0   FGR/FGR   0 1 0 9 8

ISBN: 978-0-07-149886-9
MHID: 0-07-149886-9

This publication is designed to provide accurate and authoritative information in regard to the subject matter covered. It is sold with the understanding that the publisher is not engaged in rendering legal, accounting, or other professional service. If legal advice or other expert assistance is required, the services of a competent professional person should be sought.

—From a declaration of principles jointly adopted by a committee of the American Bar Association and a committee of publishers

McGraw-Hill books are available at special quantity discounts to use as premiums and sales promotions, or for use in corporate training programs. To contact a representative please visit the Contact Us pages at www.mhprofessional.com.

This book is dedicated to the most important people in my life: Lisa, Nicolás, and Alec.

Each new day we spend as a family represents an opportunity for me to express (in both words and actions) just how much I love you and how grateful I am to be a part of your lives.

Contents

Note

I have used the following terminology to describe apartment buildings: multifamily, multi-housing, income-producing properties, apartments, duplexes, triplexes, quads, rental properties, rental buildings, real estate, apartment complexes, residential and commercial multifamily properties.

At times, I use these words interchangeably but am always referring to apartment buildings in one-way or another. Also, I tend to use the words *he* or *him* instead of *she* or *her*. I am not being gender biased but am merely trying to simplify the writing process.

How to Read This Book

Because learning is accelerated when information is shared in a digestible, clear and concise manner, I've structured each chapter in a way that should facilitate the comprehension of the material. Repetition is proven to be one of the most effective methods for increasing comprehension, so this book was written in a way that reinforces these time-tested techniques. The following learning tools are used throughout this book to help the reader better understand and retain all of the information presented.

Quotes are provided at the beginning of each chapter. Some are relevant to the chapter and others are intended to be inspirational.

What You're About to Learn: precedes each chapter and highlights the material to be covered.

Defined: provides a definition of a term or phrase that was referenced in the chapter.

Lesson Learned: I share some of the lessons I've learned over time. These are lessons that come from my own empirical experiences and are relevant to a topic discussed in the chapter.

Note: Notes are observations or advice that the reader might want to consider.

Note

Chapter Summary: At the end of each chapter, a summary provides a quick overview of the most important points. The chapter summary reinforces the material one last time before moving onto the next chapter.

Acknowledgments

I would like to thank all the hard-working and dedicated staff at McGraw-Hill, including Seth Morris, Pattie Amoroso, Tania Loghmani, Anthony Landi, and Ty Nowicki. It's not uncommon to receive an e-mail from my editor, Mary Glenn, on a Sunday evening in response to an idea or question I had posed to her earlier in the day. Her commitment and dedication to her authors are remarkable and, as always, it has been my sincere pleasure to work with her again. I'd also like to express a tremendous amount of gratitude to my wife, Lisa, for her contribution in helping to edit the manuscript. Countless weekends were spent reading every word on every page. I appreciate all of your observations, thoughts, suggestions, advice and, above all, patience and time. Thanks also to Rick Garr for your editing prowess, and to Ben Goodman and Rontao Xu for reviewing the manuscript and providing such valuable feedback.

I'd also like to thank the sponsors who contributed to the Matthew A. Martinez Real Estate Scholarship. To learn more about this scholarship, go to http://www.matthewamartinez.com/Scholarship.html. A portion of all author royalties are donated to this scholarship fund.

Introduction

*There is no comparison between that which is
lost by not succeeding and that which is lost by
not trying.*

—Sir Francis Bacon

This book was written to help you become a successful real estate
investor in multifamily apartment buildings. In the pages that
follow, you will learn all about the opportunities and rewards, and also
the risks and challenges, associated with rental properties. If you never
have invested in real estate, this book will teach you how to begin. If you
already are an active investor in single-family homes or small apartment
buildings, this book will help you reach the next plateau of achievement
with larger apartment complexes. Use this book as your primer for
investing in apartment buildings and as a guide to learning how the
industry's best practitioners carry out their work. Without a doubt, both
the beginner and the experienced investor will benefit immensely from
reading *Investing in Apartment Buildings*.

Why do you want to own income-producing real estate? I suspect
that one or more of the following reasons may be a primary motivating
factor:

1. Greater financial security
2. Higher net worth

3. More disposable income
4. Less dependence on your day job
5. More vocational flexibility
6. More control of your personal and financial future
7. More free time to spend with your spouse, your children, or your aging parents
8. Increased financial independence
9. Greater entrepreneurial challenges
10. More fun and freedom in your life

Investing in real estate provides a tried-and-true path to achieving all of these goals over time. Whether you're a novice who is just beginning or an experienced investor who wants to get to the next rung on the ladder of success, you'll need to learn as much as possible about this business to make wise investment choices. After all, the greatest impediment to achieving one's goals is overcoming the fear of taking action, and knowledge is undoubtedly the supreme equalizer in conquering one's fears. I realize that failing to make prudent choices can result in frustration, anxiety, exhaustion, lost time, and a significant financial setback. To prepare you for the challenges you'll encounter eventually, this book explains in great detail how to invest in apartment buildings—including sourcing them, analyzing them, financing them, managing them, adding value to them, and selling them for enormous profits.

The information provided in this book is based on proven methods, techniques, and practices that I and other institutional investors and experienced real estate professionals who specialize in multifamily assets have used. Keep in mind (especially if you're a novice investor) that the methodologies used by institutional investors to acquire a 1,000-unit apartment complex are quite similar to those used by first-time investors who, for example, are purchasing a three-unit apartment building. Given that I began my real estate career investing in triplexes but now have graduated to institutional-grade properties with more than 100 units each, I have included a discussion about the full spectrum of properties, regardless of the number of units, and have made a sincere effort throughout this book to explain how deals—both large and small—work.

As you learn more about multifamily properties, you will begin to feel an increased sense of confidence, but success doesn't come easily, as this business is fraught with more than its fair share of obstacles. However, you shouldn't worry too much, because I shall not underemphasize the challenges you'll encounter. Rather, I'll attempt to paint a realistic picture of the hard-earned rewards, compromises, and commitment needed if you are to succeed. With that in mind, let's get started. The chapters that follow will provide a wealth of information that will serve as a reference manual for all your future real estate investment decisions.

If you've already started buying apartment buildings and are committed to staying the course, you may elect to fast-forward to Chapter 1. If, on the other hand, you are not committed to increasing your portfolio or have just begun to contemplate your first investment and aren't committed yet, please read on.

The Dwindling Middle Class

I'd be remiss if I neglected to implore you to act now rather than waiting and planning to begin at some time in the future. My argument for taking action immediately is outlined in this introductory chapter. Primarily, I'm convinced that the middle class—families with incomes between $40,000 and $200,000 a year—is shrinking at an alarming rate as a result of the financial burdens of our time. If you classify yourself as middle class (based on this definition), you, too, should be alarmed, but I'll explain how investing in real estate can help.

There are three distinct socioeconomic strata in the United States, and the chasm between the upper and lower groups is becoming increasingly more pronounced every day. As the income gap between these two groups widens, it highlights the inequality between those who have achieved financial prosperity and those who find themselves caught in a perpetual cycle of financial instability, poverty, and lack of opportunity. Sociologists refer to this demographic divide as the "haves" versus the "have-nots." Both of these groups are growing in numbers, but primarily at the expense of the middle class.

Burdened with excessive credit card debt and facing a precarious job market that has been severely stunted by the subprime debacle, the credit crunch, recession, the Iraq war, terrorism, and several recent natural disasters, the middle class is desperately trying to survive in this unstable environment. However, given the current economic climate, its future seems anything but prosperous. In fact, those who continue to classify themselves as members of the dwindling middle class are finding that their wages have stagnated and that their chances of reaching greater financial prosperity are seemingly negligible.

Social Mobility

Mobility is defined as the ability of families to move up and down the economic ladder. Upward mobility is the promise that lies at the heart of the American Dream. However, no longer should one consider his or her middle-class standing to be a God-given right passed down from one generation to the next. Nowadays, merely maintaining one's status has become a lifelong struggle—and rather than relying on someone else (government, corporations, or others), you must devise a sound plan of action to prosper in these changing times.

How does a member of the middle-class "elite" maintain his rank or, better yet, gain membership in the more affluent group? There are several different options for ensuring upward mobility, but one's probability of success is dramatically enhanced by the production of "entrepreneurial income" beyond the income provided by a typical 9-to-5 job. Sociology Professor Dennis Gilbert of Hamilton College explains the main distinguishing feature of the upper class as the ability to derive income from wealth rather than from work. In other words, the affluent own assets that continue to add to their income regardless of the number of hours they work. Their wealth creation continues, regardless of whether they are at work, on vacation, or asleep in bed.

I've had the privilege of speaking with Professor Gilbert to better understand his point of view. He explained to me:

Introduction

When you look at where people's income comes from, you realize the higher the income, the greater the proportion of that income is derived from assets. In other words, it's difficult to have a very large and sustainable income without getting part of that income from assets. As your income increases, a greater percentage is derived from stocks, bonds, and real estate. Most of the upper class's money comes from assets.

Even more intriguing is his notion that receiving a significant level of earned income is not sustainable. He suggests that, even if you have a comparatively high-paying job, your ability to continue generating a high income is not sustainable over the long term unless you invest a portion of that income in assets. If you are a member of the middle or upper class, you must invest in assets (specifically in real estate) if you want to maintain your standing over the long term.

The Plight of the Middle Class

Perhaps you are successful, quite content with your job, and well compensated by your employer. Perhaps your health has never been better, and you are protected by a comprehensive insurance plan. Perhaps you are blessed with a happy family life with 2.3 kids, a white picket fence, and a cocker spaniel. Regardless of your particular circumstances, the only thing that one can predict with absolute certitude is that change is imminent.

For instance, if an average middle-class family experiences a job loss, divorce, or serious medical incident, total financial disaster could soon result. Untold numbers of us know family members, friends, colleagues, and neighbors who have found themselves in this precarious situation. Elizabeth Warren of Harvard Law School writes in "The Middle Class on the Precipice: Rising Financial Risks for American Families" for *Harvard Magazine* that, "During the past generation, the American middle-class family that once could count on hard work and fair play to keep itself financially secure has been transformed by economic risk and new realities. Now a pink slip, a bad diagnosis, or a disappearing spouse can reduce a family from solidly middle class to newly poor in just a few months."

If you, too, are concerned about these rather troublesome twenty-first-century realities, then attempting to answer the following questions honestly might prove worthwhile:

- What can I do to ensure that my family doesn't struggle financially?
- How can I secure a firm middle-class footing and/or financial independence to avoid living from paycheck to paycheck?
- How do I prevent financial ruin and buffer my family from the ebb and flow of economic and personal uncertainties?

In other words, what can be done to prevent so many people from experiencing a perilous downward economic slide, and what can be done to prevent economic ruin should they lose their jobs, their spouses, or their good health (the three most prevalent negative economic influencers of our time)?

The Solution: Passive Income

Most individuals start investing in real estate because they perceive it as a path to wealth and financial freedom that will permit them to no longer need to work a day job. You can achieve financial freedom by creating a passive income stream that is large enough to cover your ongoing expenses, or you can achieve it by having a large enough "nest egg" to enable you to live off the proceeds from the interest earned each year. Income-producing real estate (specifically from apartment buildings) can provide a healthy income stream for you and your family during good times and bad. Apartment buildings are unique assets that can generate significant passive income for the rest of your life. Passive income is the profit created from rental activity and is one of the primary benefits of owning such valuable assets. One of the goals of multifamily ownership is to buy apartment buildings and manage them properly so that they generate a profit each year (i.e., they have positive cash flow). When you achieve a stabilization of your portfolio, apartment buildings can provide a sufficient financial cushion and protection should you fall victim to any of life's less favorable "chances."

Introduction

I recently met with the owner of a 50-unit apartment complex. He was 82 years old and quite frail because he had suffered a stroke a year earlier. He had owned the property for 30 years and had paid off the mortgage. Since it was generating $15,000 in positive cash flow each month, he was able to sleep well at night, knowing that his wife could live off the income from the property should he pass away. This is why passive income from apartment investing is so coveted.

Income Defined

There are three basic categories of income: earned, portfolio, and passive.

Earned income is income derived from the hours one exchanges for financial compensation. For example, your job at McDonald's or a Fortune 500 company provides you with earned income in exchange for 40 hours of your time every week.

Portfolio income is interest income on bank deposits, dividends from owning shares in publicly traded companies, or capital gains from the sale of stocks or bonds. For example, you can place $1 million in a bank account and earn 5 percent interest each year.

Passive income is, for the most part, derived from the ownership of rental property, although authors' royalties and income generated from owning patents or license agreements are other forms of passive income. Passive income includes all income generated from rental real estate investments, regardless of how active the investor is in managing the properties. For example, the income you generate from owning an apartment building would be considered passive income.

The Middle Class Defined

By definition, the middle class consists of individuals who have a certain degree of economic independence but not a significant amount of social influence or power. It refers to people who are neither at the top nor at the bottom of the social hierarchy.

By some estimates, the middle class represents approximately 47 percent of the total population in the United States. Because household income is a commonly used indicator of class, all households with an annual income between $40,000 and $200,000 (as previously mentioned) could potentially classify themselves as middle-class.

According to Joseph Kahl and Dennis Gilbert, authors of *The American Class Structure: A New Synthesis*, the American class structure is categorized this way:

Upper

Capitalist class, 1 percent: heirs, CEOs, entrepreneurs, and politicians. The main distinguishing feature of the members of this class is their immense wealth and power. They have the ability to derive income from wealth rather than from work.

Middle

Upper middle class, 15 percent: professors, attorneys, journalists, scientists, professionals, and corporate executives. The main distinguishing feature of this group is its amount of advanced education.

Middle class, 32 percent; mostly white-collar but some blue-collar-based employment; semiprofessionals and managers.

Lower

Working class, 32 percent: closely supervised clerical and blue-collar workers in highly regimented and menial positions. Routine and lack of a college education are the hallmark features of this group.

Working poor, 15 percent: people at the bottom of the occupational strata; minimum-wage janitors, cashiers, fast-food employees, and so on. They often need to work several jobs to support their families; many are first-generation immigrants from developing nations with little or no education. Many others are single mothers without much formal education.

Underclass, 12 percent: the most disenfranchised group of all. They may not even participate in the labor force; many are disabled or rely on government assistance to meet their basic needs.

Note: Some of these classes overlap, bringing the sum to more than 100 percent.

The Importance of the Middle Class

Why is the middle class so important to the overall prosperity and economic stability of our country, and how does this group ultimately affect your own well-being? Few economists would disagree that the middle class is both the bedrock of our economy and its economic engine, for the middle-class population as a whole is the greatest consumer and driver of our nation's economic output. Moreover, the professional middle class or upper middle class is the most influential group in our society, given that professors, economists, journalists, writers, and many politicians (who by profession are uniquely positioned to disseminate their views to the masses) are quite effective in shaping public opinion. This group also serves as a system of checks and balances on the actions of the upper class by tempering its members' activities should they do anything that is overtly dubious.

If the middle class was dramatically reduced in size (say, from 47 to 27 percent of the total household population), the results would be disastrous. For example, our country's ability to purchase automobiles, real estate, electronics, household goods, financial services, health insurance, and other goods and services would be severely threatened if this social stratum were to shrink in numbers (assuming that the changes result in a much larger lower class rather than a much larger upper class). A shrinking middle class would lead to higher unemployment rates, greater poverty, increased crime, and a host of other undesirable and unwelcome outcomes. Also, the loss of much of the American middle class would create a void in our political system that could potentially place too much power in the hands of the upper class.

Comparatively speaking, most third-world countries are known for having a relatively small upper and middle class and a large underclass. It would be wise to avoid duplicating this type of class ratio here, because the vast majority of these nations are also characterized by unstable economies, crumbling infrastructures, pervasive poverty, inadequate government services, and the concentration of political and economic power in the hands of an elite minority. If the top 1 percent of our population—economically speaking—were to gain control over the political and economic power in our country (as is the case in most third-world nations), it would be detrimental to the vast majority.

The Middle-Class Dilemma

According to Robert Frank, the author of *Richistan* and a columnist for the *Wall Street Journal*,

> Median incomes for American households fell for the fifth consecutive year, and families are now earning $3,000 less than they did in 2000 (adjusted for inflation). America is quickly becoming a more unequal society. Today, the richest 1 percent of Americans controls more than 33 percent of the country's total wealth. There's a huge gap that's opened up between the rich and everyone else. The rich have become more financially and culturally removed from the rest of America. Wealth disparities have grown between Richistan (the wealthy) and the rest of the United States.

Perhaps former North Carolina Senator John Edwards more accurately describes the current state of affairs:

> We live in a country with two Americas. To which do you belong? One is comprised of the affluent and the other comprised of everyone else. One America is constantly struggling; it's where poverty is rampant and health care, education, and a promising future are nonexistent. There are two school systems in America: those who can afford an elite private school and those who must settle for the public school system that is lacking in so many ways. The political system is now rigged to help the rich, which makes a journey like mine, from modest beginnings to the middle class and far beyond it, much harder than it once was.

Some sociologists assert that any reference to a two-class system (the rich versus the poor) oversimplifies matters, but in my opinion, this distortion is effective in highlighting the enormous disparity that currently exists, as this concern is commonly shared by millions of individuals throughout our country.

Introduction

According to reports in *National Review* and the *Washington Post*, Barack Obama is able to relate to the average middle-class family because of his own humble beginnings. "We were still struggling with all the student loans we had to pay off after law school, because neither of us was rich," he said. "Our parents couldn't provide us with all that education. We had to borrow. We hadn't started a college fund yet for our kids. We hadn't started saving for retirement. We had some credit cards we had to deal with. We were living in a small condo that was getting a little too small for our two kids." Barack's wife, Michelle, added: "The only reason we're not in that position [a struggling middle-class family] is that Barack wrote two best-selling books. . . . It was like Jack and his magic beans. But up until a few years ago, we were struggling to figure out how we would save for our kids."

Edwards, Clinton, and Obama feel strongly that the current tax legislation is far too beneficial to the affluent and unjustly favors the wealthy. To fix the imbalance, they would begin by repealing the current tax cuts for households earning at least $200,000. In fact, both political parties recognize the plight of the middle class as an imposing future challenge. Even Republican former governor of Massachusetts Mitt Romney agrees that the middle class is feeling "pinched." Romney prefers to make individuals more responsible for their own financial destiny, but he knows that the government must also help. For example, he proposed that gains from investments made by households earning less than $200,000 annually be exempt from taxes. Similarly, John McCain believes that middle-class American families need lower taxes, too. "It is time to cut $60 billion in taxes for middle-class families. It's time to cut wasteful spending, support economic growth, and keep taxes low. It is time for Washington to work for our families and not special interests," said the senator from Arizona.

In an article for the *New York Times*, Jared Bernstein, an economist with the Economic Policy Institute in Washington, D.C., refers to the Bush administration's policies as YOYO ("You Are On Your Own") economics: "A lot of people feel they are working harder and smarter, yet their slice is not growing much at all. It is meaningless to middle- and lower-income families to say we have a great economy, because their economy looks so much different than folks at the top of the scale, because this is an economy that is working, but not working for everyone."

Future legislation could improve your chances of creating a better life through real estate investing, although I am not endorsing political candidates here. That is for each citizen to weigh for him- or herself.

To put matters into better perspective, consider the following reports from ABC News, *Harvard Magazine,* the *Washington Post,* and *BusinessWeek*:

- Thirty-seven million people in America live below the poverty line. The Census Bureau defines poverty as a family of four living on approximately $20,400 a year.
- Forty-seven million individuals, or more than 15 percent of the population, live without health insurance. And the decline in employee-based coverage (companies providing health insurance for their employees) is increasing every year.
- As many as 28 million Americans don't even have bank accounts.
- More Americans last year filed for bankruptcy than filed for divorce or graduated from college (1.5 million versus 1.1 million and 1.2 million, respectively) . . . the segment of the population that suffered most was middle-class families.
- Middle-income neighborhoods in the nation's 100 largest metro areas have declined from 58 percent in 1970 to 41 percent in 2000.
- CEOs of large corporations made more than 400 times as much as the average factory worker. In the past decade, CEO compensation climbed by an unprecedented 340 percent. As the market declined during the past few years, shareholders' losses mounted, yet executives continued earning extraordinary compensation packages. Some companies even awarded significant stock options despite a lackluster performance by the individual(s) at the helm.

According to *Time* magazine (November 12, 2007), the CEO of Merrill Lynch, Stan O'Neal, resigned on October 30, 2007, after his firm posted a $7.9 billion loss as a result of Merrill's investments in the subprime mortgage market. Nevertheless, O'Neal received a $161.5 million golden parachute upon his departure. Today, great wealth is celebrated

Introduction

lavishly as real estate tycoons, oil barons, hedge fund managers, and CEOs of corporate America spend billions on extravagant excesses and luxuries and demand larger and more outrageous compensation packages. But it was not always that way. In fact, Mitt Romney's father, George Romney, refused a $100,000 bonus from his employer, American Motors, in 1960. The *New York Times* reported in "2 Candidates, 2 Fortunes, 2 Views of Wealth" that he had told the company's board that no executive needed to make more than $225,000 a year, and the bonus would have put him over that threshold.

- While the income of the top 1 percent of taxpayers rose by 59 percent from 1995 to 1999, that of the bottom half increased by only 9 percent.
- As Robert Frank reported in *Richistan*, the richest 1 percent of Americans in 2004 were earning about $1.35 trillion a year—more than the total national income of France, Italy, or Canada.
- College tuition has steadily increased more rapidly than the rate of inflation, and the affordability of college has become a chronic issue for the lower and middle classes. According to the Advisory Committee on Student Financial Assistance, financial barriers will prevent nearly half of all college-qualified high school graduates from attending a four-year college. More than 400,000 students in 2007 encountered financial hardships that made a four-year school beyond their reach.

Not only do those in the middle class feel that they aren't making much financial progress, but they also have begun to feel less secure about working in corporate America. The Pension Benefit Guaranty Corp. (PBGC) projects that 75 percent of all the pension plans it guarantees are underfunded by a total of $95 billion. IBM, Ford, GM, ExxonMobil, Pfizer, DuPont, Alcoa, and numerous other Fortune 500 companies lack sufficient funds to meet their obligations to their retirees.

With corporate pension plans, social security, and other government entitlement programs becoming depleted or obsolete, middle-class citizens are burdened by new and more ominous financial challenges as their security nets are taken away. These obstacles are creating a tipping point that undoubtedly will result in the demotion of many to a lower rung in our class system. Could that possibly happen to you some day?

Let me reiterate that I certainly am not suggesting that the government mandate an equitable redistribution of wealth (also known as the Robin Hood doctrine in some circles) or that socialism is a superior alternative to capitalism. Each citizen's financial well-being is something for which he or she is personally accountable, and that is a fundamental tenet of our capitalist system. Alternative systems would lead to the creation of a financially dependent society that ultimately would lack the necessary motivational levers to be sufficiently productive in today's competitive global economy. Nevertheless, the distinction between poverty and affluence in our country is becoming so great that most fear that the middle class will suffer tremendously in the decades to come.

Economic inequality is greater than it has been since the Gilded Age (1865–1929). And the middle class is clearly not faring as well as it has in the past. The income of the median family has risen by only 22 percent since 1977. However, between 1947 and 1977, it increased by 102 percent. According to data from the IRS and the Economic Policy Institute, members of the middle class were, indeed, more likely to ascend the economic ladder 30 years ago and much less likely to do so today. In contrast, the rich keep getting richer—their income gain during the past 30 years was a stellar 465 percent!

The notion that any person who works diligently will get ahead has, in my opinion, given Middle America false hope. As you can see from the information provided here, this is just not the case anymore. We live in a different world from the one our parents and grandparents once called home, and, in all candor, we need to awaken to today's new economic and social reality.

Invest in Real Estate

Real estate investing is one of many wealth-creating options that you can pursue in your quest to solidify or surpass your middle-class status, ensure your financial security, and/or create generational wealth that will help not only your immediate family but perhaps even several generations that follow.

More millionaires have made their fortunes in real estate than in any other business. In fact, the IRS reports that 71 percent of all Americans declaring $1 million or more on their income tax returns during the past 50 years were in real estate or related activities. Indeed, real estate can be extremely lucrative and has proven to be the most statistically likely way to achieve financial independence.

According to CNN/Money, the number of households with a net worth of at least $1 million (excluding primary residences) increased to an all-time record of 8.9 million in 2007. Millionaire households had an average net worth (excluding their primary residence) of nearly $2.2 million, of which more than $1.4 million was in liquid (readily accessible) assets.

More than 50 percent of the millionaires surveyed by CNN/money said that their financial success was the result of long-term wealth accumulation, and real estate remains the primary means of that wealth accumulation for many of these families. In fact, 46 percent of those surveyed owned investment real estate.

According to author Robert Frank, the newest members of Affluent America (many of the families who live in the counties with the largest number of millionaires) did not inherit their wealth; instead, *they were middle-class citizens who made their fortunes by owning assets such as stocks, bonds, and, of course, real estate.* According to Frank, the über-rich "don't buy mutual funds; they buy timber land, oil rigs and office towers." This, more than anything else, should give you hope for a better way of life, given what you will learn in this book.

The Benefits of Real Estate

As I've stated, real estate is a tangible asset that has the potential to produce passive income and appreciate over time. If you're searching for a brick-and-mortar investment opportunity, real estate is your best option. Like other investments, real estate undoubtedly will be affected by the ups and downs of economic cycles (as it most certainly is in today's down cycle), but well-located, well-managed apartment buildings offer enduring value. Also, real estate has historically generated attractive returns compared to other equity investments. Finally, you control 100 percent of the investment, as opposed to buying stock in a company, where you have little control or influence over the company's activities.

Diversification

I'm not proposing that you invest only in real estate. Rather, you must understand that including real estate in your portfolio will help you as an investor increase your diversification and allow you to participate in an asset class that complements the stock and bond markets. Diversification is one of the critical methods employed to achieve success. Because movements in the real estate market historically have had a low correlation with movements in the stock and bond markets, many investors consider real estate a key component of a fully diversified financial plan.

Staying Ahead of Inflation

Real estate also provides protection from the erosion in earning power caused by inflation. For example, if the interest rate you earn on your capital is equal to the inflation rate, your overall rate of return will be neutralized. Ideally, the goal is to invest in assets that stay substantially ahead of inflation. Real estate is generally considered an investment whose returns will, more often than not, exceed the rate of inflation— and certain investments, such as apartment buildings (when the techniques you'll learn in the book are applied), may provide substantially greater returns.

Wealth Accumulation

For generations, wealthy individuals and institutions with vast financial resources have invested in institutional-grade multifamily real estate. These investors have been seeking to preserve their capital, achieve superior returns, and increase their wealth. As discussed, real estate can provide a substantial passive income stream and is one of the best means for accumulating wealth. Passive income from rental properties can augment your earned income while you continue to work for someone else. Eventually, you could be making enough from your rental properties to be able to freely elect whether to continue working for a wage. At that point, you will decide to work because you love it or decide to quit because you no longer require the income from your day job to sustain your standard of living.

You could invest in many different types of real estate assets, including multifamily (apartments), retail (shopping centers), office, and industrial buildings (warehouses). This book will deal primarily with multifamily assets. In particular, I will discuss how to buy them, where to find them, how to manage them, how best to improve their value, and how ultimately to profit from them through what's known in our industry as a "capital event" (more on that topic later in the book).

Is This the Right Time?

Timing the market is impossible, so I never try to do it. Instead, I merely attempt to buy very good value, regardless of the prevailing conditions. Buying outstanding value is the most important factor in your future success as a real estate entrepreneur, no matter what advice is being offered by the so-called real estate gurus on late-night infomercials. Nevertheless, great fortunes in real estate or any other industry are often made during times of economic distress—in particular, when market corrections, like the current one, dramatically undervalue assets.

Down (Market) Cycle

Bill Gross is the manager of Pimco, the largest bond fund, with nearly a trillion dollars in assets. He was interviewed by the *New York Times* and commented that, "The current crisis feels different—in both size and significance." Given that Mr. Gross has lived through a number of economic cycles, his evaluation of this particular one should be noted. By the way, he plans to use some of his firm's $50 billion in cash to go "bargain shopping" during the next few years. On March 25, 2008, the *Wall Street Journal* reported, "Lenders describe the current situation as the worst since the Great Depression." One of the greatest beneficiaries of real estate cycles is Sam Zell, the founder of Equity Group Investments. He is the largest landlord in the country, owning more than 200,000 units from coast to coast. The very shrewd Mr. Zell acquired a massive portfolio of undervalued properties in the market crashes of the early 1970s and late 1980s. Depressed valuations allowed him to purchase real estate assets at a fraction of their true value. He managed to acquire apartment buildings from banks that had inherited properties from landlords who defaulted on their loans. He offered the lending institutions a percentage of the upside in the form of equity in his deals, and in turn the banks (really the Resolution Trust Corporation) provided him with an abundant selection of distressed apartment buildings at steep discounts. Zell built his fortune during the down cycles, so much so that he is known today as the grave dancer because he profited immensely during the bursting of real estate bubbles and it was said that he would dance on the graves of other people's mistakes.

When the market makes a dramatic correction and valuable real estate assets can be purchased at substantial discounts, be prepared to go shopping for the best deals you can find. The odds are in your favor that real estate assets will be selling at discounted prices every 10 to 15 years, and when the real estate market finally does recover (which historically is inevitable—and it seems as though the down cycles are shorter each time), your portfolio will profit from the smart, patient investment decisions you made when everyone else was in panic mode.

Unfortunately, most unsuccessful investors subscribe to the herd mentality, buying when everyone else is buying and selling when everyone else seems compelled to sell. There's not much upside to be gained when you follow the herd! The secret to success in real estate is to buy when everyone else is selling and sell when everyone else wants to buy. Being a contrarian undoubtedly will test your resolve, since you will be doing the exact opposite of what the rest of the market is doing. But stay the course, because real fortunes are made during such times.

You must remember that more real estate fortunes are made in down markets than are made during presumably prosperous ones. Don't believe me? Just ask Sam Zell.

Introduction

Adjustable-Rate Mortgages (ARMs), Home Equity, and Second Loans

The typical family with an ARM will see its mortgage payments rise by $10,000 a year, according to the Center for American Progress. It is estimated that about 2.8 million homeowners will have the payments on their subprime mortgages reset higher in 2008 and 2009. If these homeowners can't afford the new payments or are unable to refinance because of the significantly tighter mortgage market, they are likely to become renters again.

In addition to the primary or first loan, many home buyers took out second loans to bridge the gap between the first mortgage and the purchase price. Moreover, when home values soared, homeowners withdrew money from their homes in the form of home equity loans. As a result, not only are ARMs going to wreak havoc in the real estate market, but second loans (both piggyback and home equity loans) will also negatively influence homeownership and add to the mortgage crisis. Equity loans reached a historical high of $1.1 trillion in 2008. Any additional debt will decrease the equity an owner has in his or her home and make it more challenging for the homeowner to make their mortgage payments.

More than 1 million American properties entered foreclosure in 2007, and it is estimated that many more will do so in 2008, 2009, and 2010. A significant number of these foreclosures were rental properties acquired by speculators. When the lenders foreclose on these assets, the tenants typically are evicted. In fact, according to the *New York Times* on November 18, 2007, the Mortgage Bankers Association reported that 12.5 percent of foreclosures are non-owner-occupied. As many as 2.3 million households may move back into the rental pool as a result of out-of-reach mortgage payments on reset adjustable-rate mortgages, according to Will Balthrope, senior director of Marcus & Millichap in Dallas, as quoted in www.ciremagazine.com. This significant displacement is hardly talked about but will most certainly benefit (in terms of greater rental demand) owners of rental properties for years to come.

USA Today reported in April 2008, "The demand for low-cost apartments is soaring. In some cities, those rentals have become so scarce or hard to get into that one-time homeowners either move in with relatives or leave town . . . . Many economists are calling this the most serious financial crisis since the Great Depression."

Condo Conversions

Not long ago, I received the following e-mail from a condo conversion developer who was in default on his loan:

> The appraised value of my property is $32 million, but I'm willing to accept a price of only $18.5 million and forfeit all of my equity in the deal for a quick sale. You can buy this property for only 57 cents on the dollar! Are you interested?

The number of e-mails and phone calls I have been receiving from condo converters who need to sell to avoid foreclosure has risen dramatically. Developers who entered the market too late are now motivated to sell their properties, and superbly promising investment opportunities are available for investors who have the means to acquire them. In fact, I represent several private equity firms that have acquired billions of dollars worth of real estate assets during the past few decades. They, like Sam Zell, have been patiently waiting on the sidelines and have only recently started buying—and will buy only after the market conditions have become more favorable. They are raising several hundred million and in some cases billions of dollars to acquire failed condo-conversion projects in the markets that have experienced the greatest downturns. Their plan is to revert these projects to rental apartment buildings, hold them for the next five to seven years, and then sell the stabilized properties or convert them for handsome profits when the market rebounds.

Positive Future Trends

- The crisis that started in the market for mortgage debt shows few signs of abating any time soon. In fact, the next few years should be one of the best times to acquire multifamily properties since the last crash in 1989.

Introduction

- Given the demise of the subprime mortgage market, the subsequent credit crunch, and the implosion of the condo market, the days of compressed cap rates and stiff competition from condo converters are all but over.
- According to the *New York Times* in "New-Home Sales Plummeted to 12-Year Low in November," during the summer of 2005, annual sales of new homes reached a high of 1.39 million. Since then, sales have dropped by 53.4 percent. This decline represents the steepest drop since the housing bust of the early 1980s.
- Future demographic trends will favor apartments, as nearly 72 million echo boomers (offspring of the baby boomers) will complete their college years during the next decade. Homeownership is expected to be lower for this generation than for previous generations, with the result that when these people leave college, they will enter the rental market. Marcus & Millichap predicts that average national apartment vacancy rates will hover around a healthy 5.8 percent in 2008 and 2009. Average cap rates in primary markets are expected to climb at least 50 to 100 basis points to 7 percent or more this year.
- The president of the Dallas, Texas, Habitat for Humanity, Philip Wise, launched a Land & Development Fund to finance and develop property because of the more favorable market conditions.

Investor demand for apartment buildings will continue to strengthen because these assets remain attractive investments that can generate a stable and reliable cash flow and an above-average return, especially while the volatility in the stock market persists. If you are buying for cash flow and have been patiently searching for moneymaking opportunities during the past few years but haven't been finding them, your perseverance will be rewarded soon with an ample supply of properties that should produce an above-average return on your equity. In fact, barring the shadow effect (a shadow inventory is created by overbuilding of single-family homes and condos or by the attempted conversion of apartment buildings to condos), the healthiest apartment markets throughout the country are experiencing lower vacancy rates, higher rents, fewer concessions, and increased demand.

If you've been thinking about starting your real estate investing career or adding more properties to your existing portfolio, this is a great time to do it. You should be able to acquire some outstanding properties at very favorable cap rates during the next few years. You don't need to be an institutional investor to reap the benefits of a down market. By duplicating their investment strategies (albeit on a smaller scale), you'll realize above-average returns. If you want to reap these significant financial rewards, follow the lead of seasoned investors who have lived through several market cycles and are now deploying their capital to buy as many discounted apartment buildings as they can find during this down cycle.

About the Author

I've spent several years sourcing, underwriting, managing, financing, acquiring, and disposing of multifamily apartment buildings, both for myself and with institutional investors. During this time, I've experienced both the highs and the lows of real estate entrepreneurship. Tenants who were delinquent with their rents, underperforming property managers, capital expenditures that exceeded my original estimates, banks that refused to finance my projects, and vacancy issues that lingered longer than anticipated have all tested my resolve to stay the course. Nevertheless, I've gained a tremendous amount of satisfaction and fulfillment from owning income-producing properties, and real estate has undoubtedly provided me with unique opportunities. More important, I'm truly passionate about what I do and thankful for the opportunity to do it. And that, for the record, is the ultimate definition of vocational success.

Before acquiring my first apartment building almost a decade ago, I searched bookstores for information that would prepare me to become a successful real estate entrepreneur. I was eager to get started, but I had a seemingly endless list of questions that needed to be answered. Unfortunately, most of the books I found online or in bookstores had been written by self-proclaimed real estate gurus who promoted instant wealth creation. They wrote exclusively for individuals who were desperate to achieve the American dream of overnight financial prosper-

Introduction

ity. Those late-night infomercials were equally disconcerting, as they promoted a no-money-down, rags-to-riches, opportunistic approach to wealth building.

I wondered how many people really bought those CDs, videos, books, and boot camps. They probably sold millions because they were marketed to a broad audience that was more susceptible to believing in an idealistic dream if it also offered a glimmer of hope for a better way of life and an easy, fast way for achieving it. Fortunately, I also knew that hard work, dedication, perseverance, time, a bit of good fortune, and even some sleepless nights would be required.

I did, however, manage to find a few books that provided a more realistic and honest approach to real estate investing. Unfortunately, the majority of them were written by seasoned investors who were chronicling their life's achievements as a memoir-like dedication to their offspring. I personally couldn't relate to their stories (most of them were 60-year-old real estate veterans), so I decided to write my first book, *2 Years to a Million in Real Estate,* and this book for the next generation of entrepreneurs.

My qualifications are that I'm a fairly ordinary guy, probably just like you. I certainly wasn't born with a silver spoon in my mouth or with a Trump-like father who had groomed me since birth to take over his vast holdings. Reared in New England in a single-parent household as part of a humble, middle-class family, I learned to fend for myself. Perhaps that's why I'm so concerned about the middle class in our country.

A decade ago, I was working 9 to 5 in corporate America and hoping for a better way of life, especially one in which I had more control over my own destiny, probably just like you, right? Since then, I've gone on to write a bestselling book, *2 Years to a Million in Real Estate*, that ranked as high as number 10 on Amazon and has been translated into Korean; am an AOL Money Coach along with Donald Trump and Robert Kiyosaki and a spokesperson for Intuit's property management software; founded one of the largest real estate investment groups (www.landlordandinvestor.com) in the country; and have worked with numerous institutional investors (hedge funds, private equity firms, and high-net-worth entrepreneurs) to acquire, manage, improve, and ultimately dispose of institutional-sized apartment buildings—and have enough sound advice based on my own empirical experience to fill this short book. In the pages that lie ahead, I'm prepared to share with you all of my thoughts, predictions, frustrations, victories, and especially mistakes (and there were many) so that you, too, can achieve your goals, lofty or modest as they may be, as a real estate entrepreneur.

1

Multifamily Residential (Two to Four Units)

If one advances confidently in the direction of his dreams, and endeavors to live the life which he had imagined, he will meet with a success unexpected in common hours.
—HENRY DAVID THOREAU

What You're About to Learn

- What a residential multifamily property is
- What a "small" multifamily property is
- The advantages and disadvantages of two- to four-unit multifamily residential properties
- Why novice investors should begin with smaller multifamily residential properties

Multifamily housing is a form of residential property that has more than one unit in the same building. There are two basic categories of multifamily properties:

- Buildings with two to four units
- Buildings with five or more units

Two- to four-unit apartment buildings can be acquired with residential loans, however, properties with five or more units require commercial loans. Because of this, and for the ease of differentiating these assets throughout this book, I refer to buildings with two to four household units as "small" multifamily properties. Two units in one building make a duplex, a building with three units is a triplex (a triple-decker in Boston), and one with four units is a quad or quadraplex. I refer to all properties with five or more household units within a building as "large" multifamily properties. Technically, however, all apartment buildings, regardless of the number of units, are classified as *multifamily residential properties*.

The four-unit cutoff is not an arbitrary delineation mark but, rather, was created by lending institutions to distinguish between properties that individuals may purchase as their primary residences and properties that are acquired strictly as income-producing investment vehicles.

A property with two to four units is still considered by lenders as residential; therefore, there are many more opportunities to finance this category of property through conventional programs.

Multifamily Residential (Two to Four Units)

Lending institutions concluded a long time ago that it would be acceptable for an individual or family to buy a duplex, triplex, or quad and live in one of the units as a primary residence. Presumably, the rent from the remaining units would help offset the property's operating expenses and mortgage debt. They also determined that a buyer of an apartment building with five or more units would more likely be an investor, and thus a commercial loan would be required to purchase such a building. Because lenders have created this clear delineation, it's important that you understand the differences because you'll

1. Pay much less to secure financing for a small multifamily property than you will for a large multifamily property.
2. Have many more loan programs available to you when you purchase small multifamily properties.
3. Be the beneficiary of less-restrictive bank underwriting guidelines with small multifamily properties.

Residential multifamily loans for buildings with two to four units are much easier to secure, are less costly, and require less up-front capital to close. In fact, many FHA loan programs are available for two- to four-unit housing. Residential loans are fairly easy to qualify for because lenders are primarily concerned with the loan applicant's personal credit rather than the viability and profitability of the building from a purely business or rental perspective.

In my opinion, novice investors should first "cut their teeth" on small residential multifamily buildings before buying, for example, a 10-, 20-, 50-, or 100-unit apartment complex. Countless aspiring investors have approached me during the past few years searching for validation of their plans to begin with a large multifamily acquisition. They preferred to think and act *big* and to achieve higher returns more quickly. Admittedly, above-average returns are possible with larger properties; however, and contrary to conventional wisdom, they are not always achieved, because maximizing returns really depends on how you buy the property and what you do with it, not on the number of units.

The following is an e-mail from my real estate mentor, who has more than 40 years of experience in the business:

Matt,

I've been searching for properties in Florida for the past two years, and the numbers just don't add up. I can buy a triple-decker in Boston and achieve a higher return on my equity than if I buy a 50-unit apartment building down south.

I strongly advise individuals entering this field for the first time to begin with a small multifamily property and learn the best way to manage buildings, tenants, operating expenses, and property managers. Take your time, and learn this business without jeopardizing your finances. Should you make an error in judgment with a large multifamily property, you run the risk of losing everything you own. After you've achieved a semblance of competence and gained critical hands-on experience with smaller properties, you then will be in a position to determine whether you're capable of graduating to the next level.

Note: You shouldn't buy *big* until you've gained more experience! Don't be in a rush to conquer the world. Cut your teeth on smaller properties and methodically make your way up the property ladder to larger assets.

Both my real estate mentor and I own a combination of small and large multifamily properties. We also agree that owning larger buildings doesn't always lead to greater returns. In fact, it is true that smaller multifamily properties are easier to buy, finance, and dispose of when the time is right. Undoubtedly, you might make as much money, if not more, from buying a quad as from some larger properties with 30 or more units. This is evident because profiting from real estate transactions isn't completely dependent on buying large buildings—it really depends on several factors, such as where you're buying, how good a deal you were able to negotiate, and how well you're able to manage and improve the value of that particular asset.

Multifamily Residential (Two to Four Units)

Buildings with fewer than five units offer several distinct advantages:

- *Financing.* As mentioned previously, financing requirements for small properties are much more favorable. Closing costs are significantly less, and banks are more willing to lend on this kind of property if the buyer has good credit. Rental income from the non-owner-occupied units can be used in calculating the buyer's qualification ratios. Also, VA and FHA loans are available for these kinds of properties, reducing the up-front capital required for the purchase. Finally, interest rates can be significantly lower if owner-occupied financing is obtained.

- *Down payment requirements.* One can purchase a two- to four-unit building as an owner-occupant (i.e., you live in one of the units) with a relatively low down payment (perhaps less than 5 percent down, in some cases). Lower down payments are offered to owner-occupants because the risk of default is statistically much lower if the owner is residing in the property.

- *Learning curve.* Understanding every aspect of a property is critical to your success, and managing smaller properties tends to be much easier and faster to master if you have limited experience.

- *Cash flow.* Smaller properties certainly can lose money each month (like their larger counterparts), but the worst-case scenario isn't as earth-shattering. If your property's operating expenses and debt service significantly exceed its effective gross income (more on these calculations later in the book), your negative cash flow won't be nearly so large with a smaller property as it could be with a larger one. If your 100-unit multifamily building is hemorrhaging, the losses can be staggering!

- *Management.* You can manage smaller properties on your own, but you're likely to require assistance with larger multifamily buildings. Managing a property yourself will save you the added expense of hiring a property management company, and will provide you the opportunity to learn how to manage these assets at the beginning of your career.

- *Liquidity.* Because smaller multifamily assets cost less to acquire and are easier to finance, they often sell much more quickly than larger properties because the potential universe of buyers is far greater. Admittedly, quick sales ultimately depend on pricing (among other factors); however, two- to four-unit buildings tend to sell more rapidly on average (assuming that the seller is reasonable on the market's cap rate–driven price) for all the reasons previously mentioned.

From the buyer's perspective, small multifamily properties offer the distinct advantage of acquiring an apartment building as a primary residence. For instance, you could buy a triplex, live in one of the units, and use the rental income from the other two units to pay the mortgage, insurance, maintenance, and property taxes each month. Essentially, you can be living mortgage-free if you buy the property at a decent price and manage it properly. Some of the savviest investors I know started their careers in real estate by doing exactly that.

Getting Your Feet Wet before Jumping into the Deep End

Countless individuals I know purchased their first apartment buildings with a great deal of enthusiasm and even greater determination to succeed—only to realize a few months or years later that being a landlord wasn't a business they really wanted to pursue. I suspect that, after receiving phone calls from irate tenants at inconvenient hours of the day, being surprised by operating expenses that hadn't been anticipated, and having to shoulder the financial burden during the months when higher-than-expected vacancies resulted in negative cash flows, they became disenchanted with the prospect of being a landlord.

Life as a real estate entrepreneur might seem at first like a rather glamorous avocation, especially if you envision yourself driving around town admiring your vast holdings while you revel in the fact that they are producing a sizable income for you and your family. However, you shouldn't quit your day job and/or make any definitive decisions about your vocational future until you've had the opportunity to experience both the highs and lows of being a landlord. Furthermore, you should consider the acquisition of larger properties only after you've concluded that this business is one you enjoy and one that you truly want to pursue.

Chapter Summary

- Residential multifamily properties are divided into two sub-categories: those with two to four units and those with five or more units.
- Residential loans can be used to acquire buildings with two to four units.
- Commercial loans are needed for buildings with five or more units.
- Two- to four-unit properties offer several distinct advantages, including being easier to finance, with lower interest rates and down payment requirements; providing a greater number of potential buyers upon disposition; being less management-intensive; and having less overall (depending on the area and purchase price) financial risk.
- Learn the business with smaller properties and use them as stepping-stones to owning larger multifamily properties.

2

Multifamily Residential (Five or More Units)

Worry about being better; bigger will take care of itself.

—Gary Comer

What You're About to Learn

- What a large multifamily property is
- Advantages of larger properties
- Disadvantages of larger properties
- How to dissect larger properties
- How apartment buildings are graded

Investing in Apartment Buildings

As mentioned in the previous chapter, I refer to buildings that consist of five or more units as large multifamily properties because they require commercial loans to purchase them (this allows me to separate multifamily residential properties into two distinct categories). Thus, to purchase a 5-unit apartment building, just as to purchase a 10-, 20-, 50-, 100-, or 1,000-unit complex, you will need to obtain a commercial loan. Regardless of the actual number of units, owning large multifamily assets should be your long-term objective, but only after you've gained some experience and have decided to make a commitment to being a real estate investor. After all, owning a 50-unit building with 50,000 square feet of rentable space and 50 or more tenants is going to be much more time-consuming and challenging than owning a triplex with 3,000 square feet and only 3 tenants.

Just as there are numerous advantages to buying small multifamily apartment buildings, there are also distinct advantages to owning and operating larger apartment buildings. Some of the advantages include the following:

- *Consolidation.* If you own nine units in three separate triplexes, you'll have three separate roofs, backyards, front doors, driveways, and so on to maintain. It's often much easier to have all nine units under one roof.
- *Property management.* There are economies of scale when you own larger buildings. Using the previous example, you or your property manager could visit everything in one trip—seeing all nine units at once rather than having to drive to three different locations to inspect the same number of apartments. Also, as a percentage of rental income, professional management for larger properties tends to cost less. A triplex might cost you 8 to 10 percent of gross income, while a 50-unit building might cost you only 3 percent.
- *Vacancies.* One vacancy in a ten-unit building equates to a 10 percent vacancy rate. One vacancy in a three-unit building equates to a 33 percent vacancy (or more than three times as much as for the larger property).
- *Cash flow.* If the property is managed well, the resulting cash flow could yield far superior returns. That said, it's much more

challenging and could require a significant up-front and ongoing investment to maintain a larger property at steady state (i.e., 90 to 95 percent occupancy in some urban areas) while keeping all of the operating expenses in check. Ultimately, the return on your invested capital is a function of the purchase price, value-added measures, management, and other such factors, so superior returns are not necessarily determined by a property's size.

- *Nonrecourse debt.* This kind of financing does not require the borrower to assume personal liability for the loan. The loan is typically secured by the real estate being purchased, but the borrower is not personally liable. If the borrower defaults, the lender can take ownership of the property in a foreclosure proceeding, but the lender is limited only to the value of the collateral (property) being pledged. In other words, if the borrower defaults on a nonrecourse loan, the lender is likely to foreclose on the property and take control of the asset; however, the lender cannot sue you personally for any deficiencies. Nonrecourse debt is normally available only with commercial loans.

Some of the drawbacks associated with large apartment buildings are:

- *Commercial financing.* Buyers of large properties are not offered the "cookie-cutter" financing programs that are offered to buyers of small multifamily buildings. Commercial mortgages require extensive due diligence on the part of the bank and substantially more paperwork from the buyer to justify the purchase.
- *Down payment.* The down payment tends to be far greater when you buy larger buildings. Most commercial lending institutions require a minimum of 20 percent down when buying a building with five units or more.
- *Lending requirements.* These are much more stringent. Banks will spend significantly more time underwriting these deals and analyzing your projections. Lenders must know that their investments are sound. For instance, your debt service coverage ratio (DSCR) will probably need to be at least 1.2 or greater (more on this topic

later). Historically speaking, lenders on small multifamily properties conduct much less due diligence than lenders on large properties. Ultimately, a commercial lender's primary concern is with the
property's performance rather than anything else.

- *Capital improvements.* The investment required for capital improvements (particularly on large value-add deals) tends to be far
greater simply because of the number of units and the size of the
property.

- *Property management.* Management of these properties is much
more labor-intensive and might require an on-site manager. Because you may not be able to manage a large property by yourself,
you'll need to budget for this additional expense.

- *Operating expenses.* These expenses can be much greater for
larger properties if the project takes a turn for the worse. Water,
waste removal, utilities, property management, repairs, security,
and other such costs can lead to severe financial challenges if you
haven't stabilized the property. If you buy a large apartment building and are confronted with a major capital expenditure such as a
new roof, foundation repairs, or a new boiler, it can cost you tens
of thousands of dollars in just a weekend's time. You must know
the up-front investment required before you take ownership. A 10
percent cap rate property with much deferred maintenance that
needs to be addressed can quickly turn into a very bad deal when
all is said and done!

Buying Larger Buildings

When you do eventually purchase a large multifamily building, try to
divide the property into manageable blocks of units so that the lease-
up and renovation processes are easier to control. For instance, if you
acquire a property with 50 units in five buildings (each containing 10
apartments) and your vacancy rate on day one is 30 percent (or 15 units),
don't try to tackle all of the vacant units at the same time. Instead, begin
with the building that requires the least amount of work. Renovate the
vacant units in that building, make the necessary upgrades, and rent

them out as quickly as possible. By managing the process in this methodical way, you will avoid being overwhelmed by the sheer quantity of work required. Instead of thinking that you own 50 units, concentrate on 10 units (one building) at a time and get those units 100 percent rented before moving on to the next group. That said, you always must have at least one rent-ready unit in each apartment category (one-bedroom/one-bath, two-bedroom/two-bath, and so on) in which you have a vacancy available to show to a prospective tenant at a moment's notice. Never miss an opportunity to rent to someone who is interested in leasing a unit!

These same rules apply if you acquire a 50-unit building in which all the apartments are beneath one roof. In this case, instead of dealing with one building at a time, you could focus on one or two floors at a time until the building reaches a steady state. Don't spend your entire capital-improvement budget in the first 100 days. Renovate a few units, then rent them out. Then renovate a few more units and rent them out, thus slowly and prudently using the money in your capital-improvement budget to pay for the necessary upgrades and repairs. Conventional wisdom might suggest that it's easier to do everything all at once in hopes that you'll turn a property around quickly and that you can benefit from having the contractor complete the entire job all at once. You must always weigh the pros versus the cons, as each project is unique and requires its own development plan.

I've owned small duplexes and large apartment complexes that spanned an entire block. At the end of the day, I prefer larger properties (especially institutional-sized properties) only if they are managed by very competent property managers whom I trust. Moreover, I consider larger properties only if I'm able to allocate sufficient funds to capital improvements, deferred maintenance, and general unit upgrades so that the property can attract good tenants who are able to pay market rents, making it feasible for the asset to reach some semblance of stabilization. If you are able to accomplish this as well as acquire the property at the right price, success is undoubtedly within your grasp.

Note: Institutional-sized properties start at 150 units or more.

Grading of Apartment Buildings

All income-producing properties are rated by a grading system: Classes A, B, C, and D. Class A properties are the newest (typically less than 10 years old). These are properties that offer superior design, construction, and finish. They usually attract the highest rental rates.

The Class B building classification typically includes properties that aren't of the highest quality and don't have the most modern amenities, design, and finish found in Class A properties; however, the construction is more than adequate, and they generally command average to above-average rental rates.

Class C properties provide adequate construction, design, and functionality but show some evidence of deferred maintenance. They usually earn below-average rental rates.

Class D properties are the oldest properties (30 or more years old) and tend to be suffering from functional obsolescence. They typically require significant capital improvements and have deferred maintenance problems that need to be addressed immediately.

Chapter Summary

- The benefits of owning larger properties are numerous, but you must learn to crawl before you can run or even walk. That said, once you are ready for the major leagues, large multifamily properties can generate attractive cash flows and enormous returns if they are purchased and managed well.
- There are numerous benefits to owning large multifamily properties, including consolidation of management activities, ease of property oversight, and the diminished overall impact of vacancies.
- The disadvantages include more stringent financing and down payment requirements, the need for initial and ongoing capital improvements, and higher operating expenses.
- Properties are divided into four classes: A, B, C, and D.

3

Your Farm Area

The man who does things makes mistakes, but
he never makes the biggest mistake of all—
doing nothing.

—Benjamin Franklin

What You're About to Learn

- What a farm area is
- Why you should limit your property search to a single farm area
- The competitive advantage of having local knowledge
- How to grade a property's location
- The risks associated with buying properties that are not in your farm area

You need to select a location that will be your target area for purchasing properties. Regardless of the size of your team and its ability to cover expansive territories, you'll still need to focus on certain locations if you are to be successful. The geographical area (i.e., neighborhood, town, city, state, or region) in which you conduct your search for new properties is referred to as your farm area.

Becoming an expert in a specific area allows you to be intimately familiar with that location's property values, vacancy rates, comparable sales figures, market rents, future development plans, and so on. Learning everything there is to know about a particular farm area will enable you to analyze properties quickly and determine which ones offer the greatest amount of value for your investment capital.

You can make a fortune if you are keenly knowledgeable about each and every property within a 30-minute drive from your primary residence. There are enough opportunities for making a tremendous amount of money close to home—regardless of the economy, rental demand, market conditions, or interest rates.

Information and knowledge are critical in this business. I realized a long time ago that real estate is, for the most part, a local game in which the most successful investors pride themselves on knowing everything there is to know about their particular farm areas; because of this, they are able to create vast fortunes. Information is by far the most valuable commodity in real estate investing; without it, you're just another speculator.

Buying Outside Your Farm Area

In many secondary and tertiary markets located far from your chosen area, there are undoubtedly multifamily assets that are being sold at more favorable cap rates. Many of these markets are expected to benefit from future expanding populations, strong job growth, and limited new apartment development during the next decade. As a result, many investors are considering new markets because, among other positive trends, apartment occupancies and rental rates are strengthening in these locations.

In fact, I recently attended the annual meeting of the National Multi Housing Council (NMHC), and many of the speakers touted the following cities as having the highest growth potential for multifamily investors: Charlotte, North Carolina; Baltimore, Maryland; Birmingham, Alabama; San Antonio, Texas; Tacoma, Washington; and Tucson, Arizona.

Your Farm Area

Whether you are a novice or a seasoned multifamily investor, I recommend that you join the National Multi Housing Council (www.nmhc.org).

The question you might eventually ask yourself (especially if you live in a high-barrier coastal town where cap rates tend to be low and finding a property that will produce a positive cash flow with a 20 percent down payment has not been easy) is whether you should expand your farm area and consider properties in other cities, states, and regions of the country.

I've received countless e-mails from individuals asking whether they should consider buying a property in another part of the country where the acquisition costs (at least per unit) are lower and the returns appear to be higher.

For example, a California-based investor sent the following e-mail:

Hi Matt,

I purchased your book, *2 Years to a Million in Real Estate,* and enjoyed reading it. I'm still trying to assimilate the wealth of material! I'm sure you get this question often from aspiring investors who live in expensive markets such as mine—Los Angeles. Namely, how to get into the market after it's already had a major run. I have trouble finding properties with decent cap rates out here. Even looking around the country, it's challenging. Charlotte, Austin, Albuquerque, Atlanta, etc., have better cap rates but provide little cash flow. And, of course, they are out of state. What do you usually tell investors like me in overpriced markets? I'm wondering if investing out of state makes any sense.

Thanks,

Richard

Los Angeles, CA

Investing in Apartment Buildings

Admittedly, chasing higher cap rates (the yield on your investment) and bigger properties in faraway states can be rather tempting. Perhaps you have targeted some of the high-growth cities listed earlier and are receiving daily e-mail updates from LoopNet about properties in these locales. After all, you might be able to purchase a 20- or 40-unit building in a secondary or tertiary market a few hundred miles from your home for the same price as a 3- or 4-unit building in your hometown or current place of residence. Many novice investors are extremely eager to grow their portfolios and improve their cash flow from each of their properties. You also might be convinced that larger buildings provide better returns, right?

Web site: www.loopnet.com

Think twice before pursuing the allure of bigger properties especially if they are located outside your comfort zone (i.e., your farm area). Don't sacrifice your geographical expertise for what you perceive as an opportunity in areas with which you lack familiarity.

In other words, never chase better cap rates if they are out of town! If you're considering the purchase of a property in an area outside your farm area simply because it offers a 1, 2, or 3 percent higher yield, you might want to reconsider. The more favorable returns that you initially anticipate might actually result in a much worse financial outcome given the uncertainties of managing the property from afar. The risks associated with acquiring and managing multifamily assets outside of your farm area are so great that novice investors should try to avoid this mistake.

In fact, I don't know many nonprofessional investors who have purchased apartment buildings outside their farm areas and had a positive outcome to share about their experiences. However, I have an unlimited number of anecdotes to share with anyone who is willing to listen about individuals who failed miserably in trying to turn a profit on a property they acquired in an area that they knew little about.

Personally, there are only two states in which I would contemplate buying properties right now; I spent the majority of my life in one of them and currently reside in the other. I'm intimately familiar with both locations, travel between the two on a regular basis, and am confident that the property managers who assist me with the day-to-day supervision of my investments will perform to my satisfaction.

The following is another e-mail from an investor considering an out-of-state purchase:

Matt,

I have a question to ask you. I live in Chicago and work for a major corporation. Currently, I own an investment property in Chicago, but I would like to buy some investment property in Austin, Texas, as I have heard this is an up-and-coming area. I am looking for a good deal and want to know if it is better to buy closer to home where I can check up on the property from time to time or buy down there in Texas.

Thanks,
Chris
Chicago, IL

I have a very good friend (who also happens to be a savvy real estate investor) who spent 15 months searching for better yields on properties in secondary and tertiary markets. He searched high and low in such cities as Columbus, Ohio; Raleigh, North Carolina; Austin, Texas; Oklahoma City, Oklahoma; Tucson, Arizona; and South Bend, Indiana. Ultimately, he decided against purchasing out-of-state properties because all the buildings he found that were worth investing in required intensive management to achieve stabilization, and he realized that overseeing the process would require an inordinate amount of travel and on-site management. Furthermore, managing a property from afar with a property manager that he did not trust or hadn't established a proven track record with was a risk that he was not willing to accept. He concluded (and I agreed) that turning around value-add deals is exceedingly challenging in your own backyard, and doing it out of state is even more difficult.

Local Knowledge

Can you really make a determination about a property's location if you're not familiar with the surroundings? For example, if an apartment building on the corner of Main and Jefferson is brought to your attention as a potential acquisition target, are you immediately able to make a judgment call regarding an area that's not located in a place where you have spent a significant amount of time? I suspect not.

If you lack familiarity with a property's location, you could be setting yourself up for failure. While the corner of Pine and Maple *in your farm area* might be an ideal location to own rental properties, you know that five miles south of those coordinates is an area that you'd never consider investing in because it is crime-ridden. Of course, you know this because it's in your farm area!

If there's a property for sale within a few miles of your home, I suspect that you'll be able to make a decision regarding the location almost immediately, right? You will benefit immensely from confining your acquisitions to a finite area, given that every town and street is unique to its specific location.

Limiting your farm area to a 30- to 60-minute drive from your primary residence will also simplify your investing strategy and improve your chances for success (especially in the beginning of your investing career). Institutional investors with the resources to hire local experts who are knowledgeable about new areas are able to own properties throughout the country and be highly competitive in the process. However, even investors with hundreds of millions of dollars to spend find themselves at a distinct disadvantage if they don't have a local presence in the places they're buying. Knowing every neighborhood, street, alley, nook and cranny in your chosen farm area is your competitive advantage. After all, you read the local papers every day, drive the streets, watch the local news, and live and work in the neighborhoods where you're considering the purchase of rental properties, and this knowledge is extremely valuable.

Speaking from Experience

I once acquired a 10-building apartment complex that was about 1,200 miles from my farm area. Unfortunately, I was chasing cap rates, and I was enticed by the perceived higher returns. I spent only one week on the site conducting my due diligence. I spoke with the tenants, the postal delivery agent, local police officers, the existing property management company, the on-site property manager, the owners of nearby apartment buildings, and other such people to gain a better understanding of the property, its locale, and its future challenges and potential. After taking ownership, I was confident that I had conducted a thorough property inspection and due diligence, and that I would not encounter too many surprises. Within two months, however, I realized that the area was not as safe as I had anticipated. Also, the on-site property manager was providing five free apartments to family members and had been reporting the units as vacant. Furthermore, he was collecting some tenants' rent in cash and keeping it for himself while reporting those units as being delinquent. Moreover, the property inspector failed to note any of the serious water leaks throughout the property. And no one I spoke to mentioned that there were two drug dealers doing a brisk business on the premises. Needless to say, these "surprises" cost me thousands of unbudgeted dollars and several months of headaches. I hired and fired three property management companies and was unable to achieve my goals for the property before selling it.

Fortunately, I learned more from that one apartment complex than I did from most of my successful ventures. It really tested my resolve to find solutions to serious problems. That having been said, Marcel Arsenault, an investor who built a real estate empire worth more than $200 million, once told me, "You don't learn how to ride a bike by falling off it. You learn how to ride a bike by staying on." Given that he has lost money on only one transaction out of more than 150 acquisitions, he should know. Everyone in this business has battle scars, but you need to win more than you lose if you want to be successful. Learn from your mistakes and try not to repeat them; learn from your successes and try to duplicate them as often as possible.

> *Lesson learned:* Victoria Holt once said, "Never regret. If it's good, it's wonderful. If it's bad, it's experience."

As previously discussed, my personal investing rule is to limit my farm area to only two cities (the city where I grew up and the one that I currently call home). In fact, I spent more than two years educating myself about the city where I now live before I began to feel comfortable making sound investment decisions there. Simplify your investment strategy and improve your chances for success by limiting your property search to well-defined farm areas. Don't spend time searching for properties in other locations. You must be vigilant in knowing everything there is to know—and when you find good value, don't hesitate to act quickly.

Grading Property Locations

One of the constants in every state in the country is that some areas are extremely desirable places to live and others are less desirable, and then there are areas that fall in between these two extremes. Property locations are ranked much like the assets themselves. The same scale applies: A, B, C, and D.

Class A areas are those that rank the highest in terms of having households with the highest average incomes, the least amount of crime, and the very best school systems. By contrast, Class D areas tend to be crime-ridden neighborhoods with the highest rates of poverty and the worst school systems. Class B areas are good, middle-income neighborhoods that are generally safe and have relatively low crime rates. Class C areas are blue-collar or immigrant neighborhoods that tend to have some challenges with crime and poverty, but certainly aren't war zones like the Class D neighborhoods.

Chapter Summary

- A farm area is a specific location (neighborhood, town, state, or region) where an investor will consider properties for acquisition.

Your Farm Area

- Institutional investors might buy assets throughout the country or the world but they, too, have specific areas in which they prefer to buy.
- It is recommended that you define the boundaries of your farm area and remain concentrated on that location.
- You must be intimately familiar with all of the properties in your farm area.
- You can make plenty of money in real estate regardless of the economic climate if you know every property within your farm area.
- Do not chase cap rates in other areas that you know little about. A property that might appear to generate a superior return can quickly become a money-losing proposition.
- Owning property outside your farm area is extremely challenging for a novice, or even a seasoned investor if you don't have trustworthy, dependable, and experienced local resources to help.

4

Value-Add Deals

There is only one thing that makes a dream
impossible to achieve: the fear of failure.

—Paulo Coelho

What You're About to Learn

- What value investing is
- What a value-add deal is
- How to find value-add deals
- Why you should *never* pay retail
- How to create additional value by increasing NOI
- How to determine a property's future value after implementing a value-add plan

I'm sure you've heard the name Warren Buffett. Not only is he ranked by *Forbes* magazine as the richest person in the world, with a net worth of $62 billion (up $10 billion from a year ago), but he is also considered the world's greatest investor. In fact, a $10,000 investment in Berkshire Hathaway, Buffett's holding company, in 1965 was worth $30 million by 2005. During the past four decades, he has built Berkshire Hathaway into a $200 billion company. According to Forbes.com, its value increased by a stunning 360,000 percent during that time.

Mr. Buffett is the consummate value investor, because he'll only consider companies that are undervalued by the market. Value investors attempt to find assets that are not recognized as being so by the majority of other prospective buyers. In determining whether to buy a company's stock, Mr. Buffett begins his analysis by posing the following two questions:

1. What is the intrinsic value of the company?
2. Is the stock selling at a 25 percent or greater discount to its real value?

Warren Buffett doesn't buy stock in companies haphazardly. Rather, he buys stocks based on their potential to generate earnings and their current undervalued price. He makes an investment only after understanding the value of a company and concluding that he can purchase the company or its shares at a significant discount to the actual value. The discount equates to a future profit (higher returns) that will eventually be realized.

While working with institutional investors who were acquiring large apartment complexes during the real estate downturn that began in 2007, I had the opportunity to meet with hundreds of developers, real estate speculators, and representatives from lending institutions who were highly motivated to sell their projects in the most expeditious way possible.

In fact, one developer in southern Florida shared the following with me during one of our discussions:

I spent my entire lifetime building a $9 million nest egg. Last year, I invested everything I had into this project. Today, I've sold only a fraction of the 400 units in the complex, and I'm losing $12,000 each day. The banks recently called in my loans, and I've declared bankruptcy to keep them at bay. I haven't slept well during the past year, and I just want this nightmare to be over. If I had acquired this property for a better price, I'd be able to rent all of the available units and at least break even on a cash flow basis. That, however, is not an option.

Lesson learned: Value investing allows you to buy assets at a substantial discount. Your profit is often made by negotiating a below-market price for the property you are considering. Also, buying at the "right" price prevents financial ruin should the worst-case scenario become a reality.

At this point, you've made the decision to buy a small (two to four units) or large (five or more units) multifamily property and have selected a farm area close to your home or in an area in which you have a geographical expertise and intimate familiarity. Now you'll need to devise a strategy for selecting a property, and you'll need to know how to add value to it. *Value is the worth of something compared to how much is asked for it.* Value can be very subjective and is difficult to determine, but, fortunately, there are many ways to measure value in real estate.

For instance, comparisons between similar properties can be made using the price per square foot, cap rate, price per unit, or gross rent multiplier (GRM).

Pipeline or Comparative Market Analysis Report

During any property search, I always create a simplified report for all of the properties under consideration. In this report, I list the property name, its address, the year it was built, the number of units, the asking price, total square footage, cap rate, GRM, price per unit and per square foot, monthly base rent per unit and per square foot, and other such information. This report allows me to compare and contrast all of my potential acquisition targets so that I can more readily determine which ones provide the best value. If you really want to get sophisticated with your analysis, you can assign weights to each criterion to arrive at a numerical value for each property. Ranking the properties in this manner will help you to determine which properties (from the ones on your list) offer the greatest value for your capital.

For example:

195 Main Street
Five units (three bedrooms and one bath each)
Asking price: $500,000
Livable square footage: 5,000
Rent per unit: $1,000 or $1/SF
Price per square foot: $100/SF
Price per unit: $100,000
Cap rate: Net operating income/asking price

(Cap rate will be discussed in more detail later in this book. The capitalization rate is one of the most accurate measures of comparison for income-producing properties.)

GRM: $500,000/$5,000 = 100

(The GRM is equal to the sales price of a property divided by the potential monthly rental income. The lower the GRM, the better the property.)

Of course, these ratios are not based on the asking price but on the final price you can negotiate for the property. If you are able to find a motivated owner and negotiate a steep discount from the original asking price, all of your ratios should be modified accordingly.

Determining Value

You can use all of the aforementioned data to determine how the properties you are considering compare to others in your farm area. It is important that you are comparing similar properties in the same general location. Assuming that location and other factors such as structural soundness and deferred maintenance are similar, your comparative market analysis should paint a very clear picture.

You should begin by touring at least 25 buildings. Refrain from making any offers until you have toured all the properties. This is a simple exercise and a worthwhile investment in your real estate education. Don't pressure yourself to find the ideal apartment building for your portfolio. Input all of the information previously mentioned into your pipeline or comparative market analysis report. This simple analysis provides you with a means for ranking the properties and better understanding your market.

The various price points can be noted, and other benchmarks can be highlighted. Because you don't want to buy at the top of the pricing scale for relatively similar products, the report should steer you in the right direction. Moreover, these critical data points will allow you to negotiate using the most up-to-date information.

Buying low is a skill that should not be taken for granted. Sourcing properties from motivated or distressed owners is critical, but negotiating the lowest possible price will get you the best possible deal.

A former business partner of mine once told me during the negotiations for an apartment building that we should strive to achieve a fair deal for both parties, that a win-win result was really best. "Why buy a property for the lowest possible price and risk upsetting the owner?" he asked. At that exact moment, I knew that he wasn't able to protect my best interests and would be incapable of negotiating the best possible deal for the use of my hard-earned capital. Every dollar you leave on the table during negotiations is a dollar that makes your investment more vulnerable and less profitable, and ultimately reduces your overall return. Every dollar you leave behind is one more dollar that may have to come from your own wallet to renovate units, make repairs, and invest in capital improvements. If you ever find yourself on the losing end of the negotiating table but you still proceed to the closing table, you'll certainly be disappointed in yourself if that property only generates a negative cash flow—especially if you paid too much for it. It's far better just to walk away from the negotiations if you're going to overpay.

Good Advice

This was one of the most valuable e-mail exchanges I've ever had with my real estate mentor. He wrote:

> You're looking at things like an investor, Matt, and that's not how to make money. Sure, you'll get a return and some appreciation along the line, provided you buy right, but you won't get the instant equity you got in Boston. I've been looking

at buildings with 30+ units in Florida, and I figured that I could buy five or six triplexes in Boston for the same money and make more. Just me continuing to think. First thing to remember is, we don't pay retail!!! That also means we don't pay the seller for future value. That said, the main thing to look for and consider is future value, but that depends on what you do to it. As I have always said, every time I sell a building, the buyer sees something I don't. Of course, sometimes the buyers are blind. I still say, and I think you're now saying it: pick your turf and know the values—not just property values, but rental values. You might find a property where all you have to do is install dishwashers and disposals to increase income and value. You may find an area that to most people is depressed, but to you has a future. I saw that in Andrew Square when we converted the church to retail and housing. Others didn't see the potential. We brought the yuppies to several areas of Boston and made a fortune.

Sometimes the market gets overheated and good value-add deals are hard to come by. The numbers rarely make sense in compressed cap rate environments. When that happens, don't chase deals in faraway places. Instead, just be patient and continue searching for opportunities. Don't force a deal that will ultimately cost you in the long run. Pass on projects that don't make sound financial sense. Look for and buy only good value.

After 16 years of actively buying, a good friend of mine sat on the sidelines from late 2004 until the beginning of 2008. He had always been an aggressive buyer, but he couldn't find anything to buy during that period. I wasn't sure what to make of it, but I certainly took notice. He was one of the savviest investors I knew, so his reluctance to buy and his eagerness to sell were more than just a little intriguing. I requested a meeting to ask about his plans for the future and his market predictions for the coming year. His response was, "After the blood starts to flow from this market, I will jump right back in and buy more. Until then, I'm happy to wait and watch properties being purchased at prices that don't make any sense. I'm waiting for all of the amateurs to get into trouble, and then I'll buy at discount prices from motivated sellers and banks."

Many investors who bought at the top of the market may not have the resources to ride out the current bust; they'll be forced to sell at significant discounts or may even default on their loans and have their properties foreclosed on by their lenders. All investors must analyze the numbers and perform a rigorous due diligence before they buy. They must know, among other things, what a property can command in rental revenue and how long it will take to stabilize. The most successful real estate investors I know have been contrarians. They sell when everyone else is buying and buy when others are selling. So when the real estate market heads south, the investors who have the cash and confidence to buy will be in an enviable position to act quickly and snap up the very best bargains.

Defined: A value-add deal is one in which the property can be improved in a way that increases the property's net operating income (NOI). If the project is well conceived, the value of the property will increase by more than the amount of money spent improving it.

Increasing NOI

The primary goal with all value-add properties is to increase the asset's net operating income, or NOI. To determine NOI, see the following analysis:

Gross potential rental revenue
Less: Vacancy and collection loss
Plus: Other income
Equals: Effective gross income
Less: Operating expenses (this does not include debt service on mortgages)
Equals: Net operating income

Value-add properties provide the owner with an opportunity to significantly increase NOI within a reasonable period of time. If this opportunity does not exist, many experienced entrepreneurial and institutional investors simply will not consider the asset because the "vig" doesn't exist, and the effort is not worth the reward.

In real estate, the vig, or the locked-in profit, is in the value-add because the property can be sold for a significant profit if the NOI can be adjusted upward after the owner takes control and implements an aggressive improvement strategy.

> *Defined: Vigorish*, or *vig*, is a Yiddish term derived from the Russian word for winnings.

If the project has enough potential, the property may increase in value by, for example, $2 million after an investment of only $500,000 is made. Investors seeking value-add, opportunistic deals often try to buy (at a discount), improve (add value by increasing the NOI), hold (typically for three to seven years for most institutional investors), and sell (at prices that meet or exceed their return requirements). The formula is not overly complex, but it is a time-tested strategy that only works when every aspect of the plan is executed properly.

Increasing Value (Case Study)

Harry Macklowe was one of the most highly acclaimed New York real estate moguls of our time. He purchased the GM Building in Manhattan in 2003 for $1.4 billion, establishing a record for the most ever paid for an office building in this country. At that time, the entire real estate industry was convinced that he had grossly overpaid; however, he was a shrewd businessman and knew that the GM Building was a true value-add deal with significant upside. He just needed to take control of the asset and implement his plan. Within a relatively short time, he gained the requisite permits needed to install a glass cube on the property's plaza (similar to the pyramid found at the Louvre in Paris).

That cube now serves as a beacon for Manhattan's Apple computer store. Apple pays top dollar for the high-visibility retail space below it. The GM Building increased in value so much that Macklowe was able to increase the property's debt to $1.9 billion, according to the *Wall Street*

Journal. This is a prime example of a visionary who understood that he could increase a property's value by executing a sound value-add plan. Although this is an example of a mixed-use (office/retail) project, it highlights what can be done to increase the value of any real estate asset when you think and act creatively. Although Macklowe eventually had to sell the GM Building to pay off his creditors, his original acquisition and value play were pure genius.

There are several things that an investor can do to increase NOI. I was once working with a group of investors from the Midwest on the acquisition of a large apartment complex in Miami. I underwrote the project on the basis that only $900,000 in capital expenditures was needed to upgrade the property and raise rents. The investors, however, budgeted $2 million because they saw things differently:

The vice president of acquisitions wrote,

> There are several things we do to every property we purchase that add certain costs to the project, but we believe they also add significant value. We completely revamp the clubhouse (new design and furniture), add a gym, add a theater, redo the model unit (new furniture, accessories, and so on), new exterior sign, landscaping, buy new furniture for the pools, and get new computers for the clubhouse. We believe these upgrades attract more residents who are willing to pay higher rents so it's worth the extra money.

Depending on the value-add strategy employed, the changes might not cost much or they might, as in the case just mentioned, cost millions.

Value-Add Deals

Value-add deals are properties where the NOI can be improved, most often by raising rents after renovations are made and/or reducing operating expenses by intense property management. Both initiatives positively influence a property's net operating income and, of course, its market value. Typically, a value-add deal is one that is not achieving its full potential, and with a well-designed capital infusion, rents can be raised, vacancy rates can be decreased, and operating expenses can be stabilized or reduced.

Value-add deals tend to be properties with problems, and that's precisely why you want them. By acquiring assets that most other investors do not want, you are able to avoid competition and extract the hidden value that your competitors were not able to envision for themselves. Always buy undervalued properties, make enhancements (i.e., a value-add), and sell at a premium. Buy from motivated sellers who haven't yet realized the true value of their property. Undervalued properties that may simply be out of favor at the time of your acquisition can be significant moneymakers. You must welcome and even embrace these types of challenges. Admittedly, it's much easier to understand the positioning and future value of a trophy property that requires little in the form of value positioning, but that's where you'll encounter stiff competition. Create value where others cannot. Try to avoid the competition and manufacture excess return. Adding value has become increasingly more important because future price appreciation no longer will come from cap rate compression. Don't pursue properties if you only think they will increase in value as the market rises; instead, buy well, operate aggressively, continuously add value, and sell at a significant profit. At the end of the day, every investment you make is a bet that you can do better than the individuals from whom you bought it.

A Case Study in Value-Add Deals

A friend of mine is a principal of a small real estate investment company that acquires distressed property, renovates and rehabilitates them, and sells them for a profit within two or three years.

- The company recently purchased a 150-unit complex in the southeast part of the country. When it acquired the property in foreclosure, it was 40 percent vacant.
- The company bought the property for $1.5 million and invested around $500,000 in capital improvements and unit renovations.
- Within 15 months, the occupancy rate had increased to 96 percent, and evictions had decreased from 15 percent to 4 percent.
- This property sold for $4.3 million after the company had held it for just two years, making about a $2 million profit!

Value-Add Deals

This case study is a good example of a value-add acquisition and redevelopment strategy. One of the best ways to succeed in this business is to buy a Class C property in a Class B neighborhood and upgrade the property from a C to a B. This strategy also works for a Class B property found in a Class A area.

You can't change the location of a property, so it's typically better to acquire a property that is well located but in need of repair. After all, you can initiate a value-add approach and significantly improve an apartment building, but there's little you can do to improve the neighborhood.

Other Income or Ancillary Revenue

There are several strategies that investors can employ to increase a property's NOI. One very effective way of achieving a higher NOI is to increase the property's ancillary revenue or "other income." Ancillary revenue is any income that isn't rent-based. This includes laundry income; storage; parking; cleaning services; pet rent; renting roof space for cell towers; sharing revenue with cable, Internet, and phone service providers; and revenue from vending machines.

Contact cable, phone, and Internet providers and inquire about their partnership programs with property owners. They typically share up to 20 percent of net revenue with the owner if your property meets their minimum unit requirement. The same sort of deal can be negotiated with laundry service companies (LSCs). The three largest LSCs are CoinMach, Mac-Gray Corp, and Jetz Service Company. They will install and service the machines and collect the revenue. You must provide the space, electricity, and water in exchange for a percentage of the revenue generated by the service. Should you decide to go this route, I recommend having a counter placed on the machines so that you can verify the usage.

Web sites:

http://www.coinmach.com
http://www.macgray.com
http://www.jetzservice.com

Form a strategic alliance with a housecleaning company and a dry-cleaning company. Market their services to your tenants and receive a percentage of their revenue, too. Because you are providing a captive audience and "exclusivity" in your apartment buildings, you should be compensated.

According to an NAHB (National Association of Home Builders) survey, garages and storage spaces were cited as important factors in choosing an apartment. Secure, safe, and clean storage areas are in high demand by renters. For example, Trachte Building Systems offers mini-storage units to renters. Adding the storage units in an existing parking garage or basement doesn't cost much relative to the added revenue they can generate (they pay for themselves in about one to two years), but they will make the property's cash flow look a lot more attractive when you sell or refinance the property.

Web sites:

---

www.securespace.biz or www.trachte.com.

Speculation versus Positive Cash Flow Properties

Speculators tend to overpay for a property because they feel that someone else will be willing to pay more for it in the near term. Alternatively, real estate investors with a value-add strategy underpay for a property because there is something wrong with it (it has "hair" on the deal), but the "problems" can be remedied with their proven expertise, initiative, and perseverance. A common practice during periods of high real estate price appreciation is for speculators to purchase income properties with the intent that rents will cover their monthly expenses for a while, and then the property can be sold for a large capital gain. As with all markets during times of fast price appreciation, and as with all market bubbles, those who enter the market first and get out first usually do well. Those who enter the market last and get out last usually don't do as well. It's just a matter of time before a speculator gets burned. Investors, on the other hand, typically do much better in the long term because they are focused on continually buying low and creating value.

Positive cash flow is critical to surviving the challenging downturns in the market. Cash flow is the money you have left each month after operating expenses and debt service are deducted from the effective gross income. Buying for any anticipated future appreciation is known in some circles as speculation. You will have plenty of upside should the market continue to flourish. But if the market takes a turn for the worse (as it often does), a good property still will "carry" itself—the property will generate enough rental revenue to cover all its operating expenses and mortgage payments. Assuming that you stick to this strategy, you will avoid having to pay out of pocket for any of the expenses associated with the asset and can maintain the property for the long term regardless of the prevailing market conditions.

A Value-Add Deal

I once acquired a property that was well located but hadn't been renovated in two decades. I knew the rents were about 35 percent below what I could get for them if the units were renovated. I also knew that the operating expenses were 70 percent of the effective gross income, but that I could get them down to 40 percent with my own property management team on the job. The current owner was paying far too much for insurance, maintenance, electricity, and water. After closing on the property, I quickly renovated the units and leased them to tenants who paid much higher market rents. I then went to work on all of the operating expenses. My plumbing company fixed all of the dripping faucets and leaking toilets, and repaired several hot water heaters. This resulted in a 25 percent reduction in the water bill. I reduced the insurance expense 22 percent by using my preferred insurance carrier. I even saved on common electricity by installing fluorescent lightbulbs with timers throughout the property. There were numerous other cost-saving and revenue-enhancing projects that when completed increased the NOI significantly and ultimately increased the value of the property. I eventually sold it for a handsome profit.

Chapter Summary

- Don't shy away from properties that are less than pristine, because they could be tremendous value-add deals.
- Value investing allows you to buy assets at a substantial discount because the property isn't in perfect condition.
- Value is the worth of something compared to the price paid or asked for it.
- Pick your turf and know the values—not just property values, but rental values, too.
- A value-add deal is one in which the property is improved in a way that increases the property's NOI.
- Adding value has become increasingly more important because price appreciation will not come from cap rate compression during a down cycle.

5

Sourcing Properties

Strive for perfection in everything. Take the best that exists and make it better. If it doesn't exist, create it. Accept nothing nearly right or good enough.

—Henry Royce, Cofounder of Rolls-Royce

What You're About to Learn

- How to work with real estate brokerage firms
- How to find the very best properties
- How to avoid the competition
- Where to obtain research reports
- How to use information to your advantage
- Why real estate investing is a local game

Investing in Apartment Buildings

There are many ways to find well-priced value-add properties from motivated sellers. At times, locating a great deal might seem as likely as finding a needle in a haystack. However, such deals do exist, but you need to know how to find them.

To locate extraordinary opportunities, you must do things that the majority of average investors won't even consider. Unearthing opportunities that aren't readily available to your competition requires that you conduct an exhaustive and thorough investigation of your target area.

Contacting all the real estate brokers (both local and national firms) that specialize in multifamily assets within your farm area is the most logical first step. Introduce yourself as a serious investor who is eager to close deals. Don't make the mistake of implying to a broker that you're interested only in "good" deals. Instead, explain your specific acquisition criteria in detail. There may be several very good local firms that can assist you, however. Table 5.1 gives the country's leading national multifamily brokerage firms.

Table 5.1

Apartment Realty Advisors (678) 553-9360 www.arausa.com	Total 2007 M-H volume in dollars: $7 billion Number of 2007 M-H transactions: 317	Regions of operation: national Most active region: southeast
CB Richard Ellis (617) 488-7237 www.cbre.com/mhg	Total 2007 M-H volume in dollars: $14 billion Number of 2007 M-H transactions: 466	Regions of operation: international Most active region: national
Coldwell Banker Commercial Affiliates Inc. (800) 222-2162 www.cbcworldwide. com	Total 2007 M-H volume in dollars: $722 million Number of 2007 M-H transactions: 1,362	Regions of operation: northeast, mid-Atlantic, southeast, Midwest, southwest, West Coast Most active region: West Coast

Colliers International (213) 627-1214 www.colliers.com	Total 2007 M-H volume in dollars: $863 million Number of 2007 M-H transactions: 31	Regions of operation: east, west, south, central Most active regions: west (Washington, Arizona), central (Texas)
Cushman & Wakefield (202) 739-0382 www.apartments.cushwake.com	Total 2007 M-H volume in dollars: $6 billion Number of 2007 M-H transactions: 200	Regions of operation: national Most active region: national
Garrison Partners Consulting (312) 670-2447 www.garrisonpartners.com	Total 2007 M-H volume in dollars: $1 billion Number of 2007 M-H transactions: 638	Regions of operation: Midwest, southeast, northeast Most active region: Midwest
HFF (Holliday Fenoglio Fowler LP) (713) 852-3500 www.hfflp.com	Total 2007 M-H volume in dollars: $1.3 billion Number of 2007 M-H transactions: 46	Regions of operation: national Most active region: N/A
JBMRA—Sperry Van Ness Institutional (813) 221-7100 www.jbmra.com	Total 2007 M-H volume in dollars: $904 million Number of 2007 M-H transactions: 34	Regions of operation: national Most active regions: southeast, West Coast
Marcus & Millichap—National Multi Housing Group (818) 907-0600 www.marcusmillichap.com	Total 2007 M-H volume in dollars: $10 billion Number of 2007 M-H transactions: 2,318	Regions of operation: national Most active regions: California, Texas, southeast

Moran & Co. (714) 444-3533 www.moranandco.com	Total 2007 M-H volume in dollars: $2.2 billion Number of 2007 M-H transactions: 32	Regions of operation: southwest, West Coast, Midwest, mountain, Pacific northwest, southeast, mid-Atlantic Most active regions: California, Dallas, Denver, Chicago, Seattle
Rock Apartment Advisors (205) 397-2200 www.rockadvisors.com	Total 2007 M-H volume in dollars: $275 million Number of 2007 M-H transactions: 37	Regions of operation: Alabama, Mississippi, Florida, Tennessee Most active region: Alabama, Mississippi
Sperry Van Ness (949) 250-4100 www.svn.com	Total 2007 M-H volume in dollars: $1 billion Number of 2007 M-H transactions: 314	Regions of operation: national Most active regions: California, Ohio, Texas, Arizona
Transwestern Commercial Services (713) 270-7700 www.transwestern.net	Total 2007 M-H volume in dollars: $2.4 billion Number of 2007 M-H transactions: 69	Regions of operation: mid-Atlantic, southeast, Midwest, Gulf Coast, central, mountain, West Coast, central Texas Most active regions: mid-Atlantic, West Coast, southeast

Source: This directory was compiled by *Multi-Housing News*.

These companies are the most active in the business, but they tend to specialize in larger properties. If you are an investor in smaller (non-institutional) properties, many of these brokerage firms have "private client groups" that deal with real estate assets with fewer than 150 units—assets that traditionally interest entrepreneurs rather than institutional investors—so be sure to ask for a representative in this group.

But your work certainly doesn't end with brokers! You must use all of the following additional resources to find the most viable and most profitable opportunities:

- Accountants
- Appraisers
- Attorneys
- Banks and other financial institutions that provide capital to acquire, develop, or upgrade real estate
- Local city planners
- Local government officials
- Real estate consultants
- Real estate (industry) conferences
- Internet/Web sites
- Financial planners
- Insurance agents
- Landlords and other real estate investors
- *Lis pendens* and foreclosure listings
- Newspapers, real estate magazines and journals
- Mortgage brokers
- Property inspectors
- Public relations (campaigns)
- Stockbrokers and wealth managers
- Title insurance agents
- Vendors: electricians, plumbers, general contractors, etc.

Having intimate knowledge of your farm area, leveraging your network to gain access to off-market deals, and using local resources that can provide valuable real estate information before competitors are made aware of it will allow you to leapfrog everyone else. Avoiding the competition permits you to be the only investor at the negotiating table . . . and that can translate into significant savings at the closing table.

Ways to Find Undervalued Properties

Real estate entrepreneurship is a numbers game. In other words, the more deals you evaluate, the more you'll make offers on and the more you'll close.

Here are just a few of the ways to fill your pipeline with moneymaking properties.

National and Local Conferences

Several organizations such as the National Multi Housing Council (NMHC) sponsor national, regional, or city-specific meetings for investors who are interested in multifamily housing. Also, your local real estate investment association (REIA) probably has monthly or quarterly meetings. Active involvement in these groups is extremely beneficial to your search because you'll expand your business network by meeting other active investors in your farm area who might introduce you to deal flow.

> *Web site:* These Web site provides a list of all the real estate clubs throughout the country: http://www.creonline.com/clubs.htm and http://www.reiclub.com/real-estate-clubs.php

Online

You can obtain information about properties that are for sale, in default, or in foreclosure by using the Internet. You also can find comparable property transactions, rents, vacancy rates, maps, and a host of other important data points, including demographics, trends, and recent sales, online. Search online databases by city, state, or zip code to find potential opportunities.

The Internet has revolutionized the way buyers search for and find investment properties. The data one can find online have made the search easier and substantially more transparent.

Online resources such as LoopNet and Craigslist provide an accessible way to obtain information on properties for sale. Then again, everyone else is also searching these sites, so you are not alone. A creative way to find new properties that aren't being marketed is to look at the "for rent" listings on Craigslist. Because everyone else is looking at the "for sale" page, you should think and act differently if you want to avoid the competition. Perusing the "for rent" section will lead to an ample supply of apartment owners with vacancies. Send them an e-mail or call them to inquire about their interest in selling their property. Perhaps they may be interested in selling now or at some point in the future. If an owner has vacancies and is searching for tenants, perhaps he or she would be willing to sell rather than spend the time required to find new tenants. Timing is everything, so leave no rock unturned.

The following is a list of additional Web sites that aggregate "for sale" listings and offer their database of properties online:

LoopNet.com: 2.5 million registered users, 535,000 listings, and 915,000 unique visitors each month make it the most widely used site for commercial properties.

COSTAR.com: 75,000 subscribers and 2.6 million listed properties, making it the largest database of commercial properties.

COMMREX.com: 25,000 members and 300,000 unique visits with 10,000 listed properties.

CIMLS.com: The commercial investment multiple listing service.
CommercialiQ.com: 200,000 listings

Also, these leading brokerage firms share their listings with the general public: Jones Lang LaSalle, CB Richard Ellis, Marcus & Millichap, Colliers, NAI Global, Cushman & Wakefield, HFF, and Grubb & Ellis.

Your Personal Network

Speak with everyone you know regarding your interest in buying income-producing properties. This should include plumbers, electricians, carpenters, general contractors, planning/zoning committee members, postal agents, and other such people. After all, you might be pleasantly surprised at who has valuable insider information regarding a superior deal.

For example, I have several acquaintances who work at For Rent publications and Internet companies that specialize in rental property advertising. They are privy to all sorts of valuable information regarding apartment complexes in my farm areas. In fact, it's their responsibility to know every apartment building, property owner, and manager in their respective markets. The field representatives must be knowledgeable about each property that is for sale, each owner who is contemplating a sale, and every property that is in default or foreclosure; this is valuable information that will also serve you well.

Mortgage Lenders

When an investor defaults on a loan, the lender might accept a short sale of the property or attempt to sell it after the foreclosure takes place. Either way, mortgage lenders are an outstanding source of opportunities for investors who want to acquire real estate assets at favorable prices.

These types of opportunities are divided into the following three categories:

1. *Distressed properties.* The owner is unable to continue paying the mortgage and is in danger of default. Perhaps he has already missed one or two months of mortgage payments.
2. *Default.* Typically the owner is 90 days late in making mortgage payments. The bank/lender considers this a nonperforming loan. The lender might sell the note, and in that case the buyer of the note must foreclose on the property to gain control.
3. *Foreclosure.* The lender has foreclosed, and the property is considered real estate owned (REO) by the lender. The new buyer has much less risk, because he can typically buy the fee-simple interest in the property from the lender. In other words, acquiring property after the foreclosure process has been completed offers the purchaser a variety of benefits. These may include obtaining the property free and clear of liens and other interests.

When the owner of a property fails to pay his mortgage and defaults on the loan, the mortgage lender that holds the paper on the real estate asset has the right to foreclose on the property. The lender should then be able to sell the property in fee-simple interest. Fee-simple interest represents absolute ownership of real property. Because most financial institutions aren't in the business of being landlords or operators of apartment buildings, they tend to be extremely motivated to remove nonperforming loans and assets that are considered REOs from their balance sheets. It is not unusual (depending on the cycle) for lenders to accept offers that are significantly discounted from the principal balance owed. The total discount amounts to the loss that the lender is willing to accept on the outstanding mortgage balance. Typically, lenders try to obtain the par value of the loan; however, if they are inundated with nonperforming loans or are otherwise pressured by the federal banking regulators (namely the FDIC) or the bank's board of directors to sell, they will reluctantly accept a discount.

As an example, let's consider a property that originally was purchased for $500,000. The owner put down $100,000 at closing and acquired a mortgage for $400,000 (an 80 percent loan-to-value ratio). If the owner defaults on the mortgage, the bank is left with a nonperforming loan of $400,000 less any principal payments the owner had made. If the bank is willing to accept an offer of $300,000 for a quick closing, you might benefit greatly from a distressed sale and become the owner of a property at an extremely attractive price (assuming the NOI and cap rate are favorable).

To find REO deals, you should have a contact within the bank who can make you aware of opportunities as he becomes aware of them, or you must know representatives at the brokerage firms that have deals assigned to them by the banks. To make inroads with a financial institution and to learn how this process works, you first should contact the bank where you conduct your own business. Introduce yourself as a customer who would like to speak with the person in charge of the REO or special assets department. The vice president of commercial lending or credit officer at smaller banks or the director of the special assets or loss mitigation division at larger banks is the person you'll want to meet. Make sure he knows precisely what you are searching for, and express your eagerness to work with him as well as your ability to close.

I once spent three weeks making several inquiries at a bank that I knew had several nonperforming loans. Unfortunately, I couldn't convince anyone at the bank to return my phone calls. Instead of leaving more messages in a futile attempt to get someone's attention, I decided to visit the bank in person and ask to speak with the credit officer or the vice president of commercial lending. I knew that he would likely direct me to the special assets division, but I first needed his introduction. As I had suspected, I didn't make it past the VP's assistant. However, the assistant redirected me to the person in charge of nonperforming loans. When I finally reached his office, I informed his secretary that the VP of commercial lending had referred me to his boss. Being able to use a high-ranking bank executive's name as a reference guaranteed a meeting with the individual I really wanted to meet. Today, I know the bank's personnel quite well and have worked with them on projects ranging from 20-unit to 500-unit apartment complexes.

On another occasion, I flew to New York City for the day, as I knew that the special assets manager for a regional bank was speaking at a real estate conference there. Although I already had called him numerous times, he had not been willing to share any details regarding specific projects that were in trouble. I approached him after the seminar and introduced myself as the person who had been calling him for the past few months. Meeting me in person and connecting a name with a face seemed to defuse any misgivings he might have had about me. Since then, he has been extremely receptive to working with me and has invited me to his corporate office to meet the other members of his team.

> *Lesson learned:* Be persistent and don't give up!

Searching Your Farm Area by Foot or by Car

If you see an apartment building that is in disrepair, make a note of the address and send the owner a letter stating your interest in buying it. If the letter is returned, you can attempt to determine the whereabouts of the property owner by inquiring with the neighbors. If there are tenants in the building, you can always ask them as well. If there's a "For Rent" sign on the property, call that number and ask to speak with the owner. Or, get the owner's name and address through the local property assessor's Web site.

Ads in Newspapers and Newsletters

Place an ad in the local paper and explain what you want to buy. Also, work with your local REIA. Most of these real estate clubs are willing to include your information (perhaps for a small fee) in their monthly newsletters. Or, they might be willing to forward your information directly to their member distribution list.

Public Relations

Public relations is a wonderful tool if you want to reach a broad audience. For example, on one occasion I was searching for a very specific kind of property (failed condo conversion developments/apartment complexes with 200 or more units that were in default). These properties are not always marketed in the traditional way. Realizing that this could pose a unique challenge, I began with a PR campaign targeted at individuals who have access to such deals. I "pitched" my story to several national and local newspapers, and I was able to secure interest from the *New York Times*, Reuters, Florida's *Daily Business Review*, and CNN. They all published a version of my story. I stated precisely how much money was at my disposal, what kinds of properties we would consider, the price range, and our farm area.

Shortly after these stories ran in these publications, I was inundated with calls from brokers, real estate investors, bankers, attorneys, and developers who either had something to sell or knew of someone who had a property that met the acquisition criteria outlined. If you are an investor in non-institutional-sized properties, I realize that obtaining "ink" from the publications just listed might not be feasible; however, your local newspaper editor might be interested in your activities if you have a unique story to share with him. If you are creative in convincing any of the staff writers that your own personal story is newsworthy, they might just write something that makes it into their publication.

The following are a few of the articles that resulted from my public relations campaigns:

> *Daily Business Review:* "Condo meltdown: private funds rush to buy failed conversion projects in bulk"; http://www.dailybusinessreview.com/news.html?news_id=46618.

CNN: "Mortgage meltdown: vulture investors"; http://money.cnn.com/ 2007/09/24/real_estate/vultures_circling/index.htm.

Reuters: "Miami condo market faces moment of truth in 2008"; http:// www.reuters.com/article/newsOne/idUSN0843045520071015.

Web site: For a list of newspapers throughout the country, visit this Web site: www.usnpl.com.

Direct Mail

Direct mail can be equally effective. Send letters to property owners introducing yourself as an investor. The property assessor's department in your farm area can furnish you with a list of owners for the category of properties you are targeting.

Research Reports

The following organizations provide commercial real estate research and statistical reports:

- CoStar: www.costar.com
- Real Capital Analytics: www.rcanalytics.com/
- Reis, Inc.: www.reis.com/
- Torto Wheaton Research (CB Richard Ellis product): www.twr.com

As a novice investor, you may not be able to afford these services; however, it's good to know that they are available. Many institutional investors use these services to complement their own analysis. Some of these organizations may offer free trial memberships, so inquire about these programs.

When I was buying three-unit apartment buildings in Boston, I was sure that the methods I was using to find these properties differed greatly from those used by institutional investors. However, now that I'm working on much larger apartment complexes, I've realized that the methods used to source these institutional deals are really no different. Whether you're attempting to find $300,000 triplexes or $30 million apartment complexes, real estate is a highly localized business, and information is always your most valuable commodity.

I've been able to find apartment buildings through many different sources, including friends, other investors, ads placed in newspapers, attorneys, mortgage lenders, property owners, and so on. Once you realize that there's an unlimited supply of great properties available to purchase, you'll also realize there's an unlimited number of ways to find them.

Chapter Summary

- To find the very best opportunities, you must conduct an exhaustive investigation of your farm area.
- Thinking and acting in ways that are unconventional will lead to extraordinary opportunities.
- Never be satisfied with the traditional means employed by your competitors who also are searching for properties. You will be rewarded with superior properties only if you work harder and smarter than everyone else.
- Leverage the Internet and your personal network to find properties.
- Real estate is a highly localized business, and information will always be this industry's most valuable commodity.

6

Buying Low

The secret of business is to know something that nobody else knows.

—A<small>RISTOTLE</small> O<small>NASSIS</small>

What You're About to Learn

- How to buy low
- What to look for in pro forma statements
- Why you must focus on cash flow
- Negotiating a better price for your properties
- Short sales
- Nonperforming loans and note sales
- Foreclosures
- Real estate owned

Investing in Apartment Buildings

As a Boulder, Colorado, business reporter once wrote: "Sell your investments that are going great, and buy what everyone else thinks is going down the tubes." The most successful and experienced real estate investors I know wholeheartedly subscribe to this contrarian investment philosophy. In other words, they do the opposite of what the majority of other investors are doing at the time—they sell when everyone else is buying and buy when everyone else is selling. They know that buying low ensures a certain amount of built-in profit, and that selling at a premium maximizes their returns. In brief, *you'll never go broke selling for a profit*, and you will always improve your chances of doing well if you buy at a significant discount.

Buying low does not just mean buying at a price lower than that of other overpriced apartment buildings in your farm area or buying at a price that allows you to obtain average returns on equity. Buying low means buying good value based on the return on capital that you hope to achieve. Buying low gives you an opportunity to generate above-average returns on your hard-earned investment capital.

Every one of your investments should be a profitable venture, and buying as low as possible increases the probability of owning a rental property that not only generates a positive cash flow, but also achieves your desired return. To achieve a positive cash flow, rental revenue plus any ancillary revenue streams (derived, for example, from laundry income, utility reimbursement, parking spaces, storage, pet fees, and other such sources) must exceed the sum of the property's operating expenses and its total debt service (more on that topic in the coming chapters).

Buying low is even more critical when rents are trending downward. If you don't buy a rental property correctly, by the time you pay the mortgage, maintenance, management, utilities, insurance, taxes, and other operating expenses, you won't have anything remaining to pay yourself! You might even have to extract funds from your own savings each and every month to carry the property. In such a case, it actually might cost you to own an "income-producing" property. Buying low is an art that the very best investors master early in their careers because they realize the importance of being good at it. They understand that a substantial profit can be made instantly at the closing table. Negotiating a favorable purchase price ensures their future success and minimizes the financial risks associated with owning the property.

Pro Forma Statements

When you are searching for an apartment building that provides outstanding value for your capital, you always should base your analysis on the property's current income and expenses (preferably the last month's rent roll and the 12-month trailing operating expenses) rather than on the owner's pro forma (projected) numbers. The owner or his broker will create pro forma financial statements to show how the property could perform given ideal conditions. However, the owner's estimates of future performance are rarely accurate; in fact, most often they are highly exaggerated. You're better off using the property's current financial statements and not the ones being promoted by the owner.

Note: A pro forma income statement is a projection of a property's income and expenses for a given number of years.

A pro forma income statement provides the potential (not the actual) income and expenses. When a property is being marketed, the owner will prepare a pro forma income statement that depicts the property's anticipated rental revenue and operating expenses given ideal conditions. In other words, the owners are assuming that, under perfect conditions, the property will generate a specific amount of rental revenue (typically the average rent per unit multiplied by the total number of units), with an acceptable vacancy rate, reasonable level of collection loss (rent money that is due but is not collected from tenants), and a nominal amount allocated to concessions (free rent or subsidies given to new tenants). Finally, the owners assume industry-accepted levels of operating expenses. Total operating expenses as a percentage of effective gross income typically range between 30 and 50 percent, depending on deferred maintenance issues, the region of the country in which the property is located, and the age of the asset.

Investing in Apartment Buildings

Always base your decision to buy on the existing rents and your anticipated operating expenses following the purchase. After you leave the closing table and are the proud owner of the property, you should be collecting an amount similar to the previous month's rent roll. Ask for a copy of the last three months' deposit slips, because the numbers stated on the rent roll can differ dramatically from the actual amount of rent that was collected. For example, let's assume that you are buying a 10-unit apartment building that is 100 percent occupied. If each tenant pays $1,000 a month in rent, the rent roll will indicate $10,000 in monthly rental revenue. However, if two of the tenants have not been paying rent for the past few months and are in the process of being evicted, the actual deposit for the previous month will be only $8,000 (a 20 percent reduction). The economic occupancy is really 80 percent and not 100 percent. Moreover, after you buy a property, some key operating expenses might rise dramatically. For example, in Massachusetts, taxes are adjusted every three years and are based on the assessed value at that time. In Florida, the taxes are adjusted annually and are based on the most recent purchase price. If you are buying a property from someone who has owned the property for the past 15 years, his taxes will be based on his original purchase price, not the new purchase price. They will need to be adjusted if you acquire the property. Also, insurance rates might differ, so you'll need to verify these numbers with a few providers before closing.

For instance, in the first few years of the pro forma, an owner might depict his property as having 95 percent occupancy with all units rented at market rates. But what he neglects to mention is that an initial investment of $1 million is required to address the enormous deferred maintenance issues that are plaguing the property. Beware of owners who provide you with sweeping assumptions about how their properties will perform in the future.

On one occasion, I was working with an investment bank to acquire a 300-unit apartment complex in Delray Beach, Florida. The trailing 12-month operating expenses were 72 percent of the effective gross income (EGI). Even though I knew that the average ratio for the area was closer to 50 percent, the broker actually showed pro forma expenses as 38 percent of effective gross income during the first year of ownership. The building undoubtedly was being poorly managed, but there was no realistic way in which the expenses could be reduced so dramatically in such a short time, and certainly not to the figure specified. To sell the property at a premium and maximize his commission, the broker's objective was to present the property in a more favorable financial light. Your objective, however, is to know which numbers are reasonable and which are merely puffery. After you've analyzed 50 to 100 of these deals and own some properties of your own, you'll be able to quickly scan a pro forma and find the false or misleading projections within minutes. Time, experience, and repetition will make you a more astute investor.

I always ask the owner or broker who drafted the pro forma, for example, how he expects a new owner to obtain these higher rents if the current owner has never has been able to achieve the amount of rents being forecasted. Brokers typically respond by suggesting that, with an aggressive property management firm in place and a small investment in capital improvements, the pro forma numbers are, indeed, achievable. It always bewilders me how some brokers can attempt to convince me of something that they know is just not possible. I recommend that you avoid this trap at all cost. Your analysis should consider only current, actual numbers and future projections that are conservatively based on what you believe are reasonable expectations for the property's financial performance. After all, why should the owner be compensated for having an underperforming and poorly managed property? If the apartment building has a 30 percent vacancy rate, operating expenses that are higher than the norm, and rents that are lower than the market, why should the present owner receive a price based on the property's future potential, given that you'll need to work very, very hard to improve his underperforming asset? Poorly managed properties deserve offers that are commensurate with their current performance. Don't pay a premium for the hard work that awaits you. After all, you'll be working diligently in the months that follow the closing to justify a discounted price.

Ultimately, it's your responsibility to question the owner's pro forma numbers and to create your own analysis based on what you believe to be accurate. You must understand precisely how a property will perform in the future to distinguish good value from a product that is being overhyped with inaccurate pro forma statements that don't depict the property's current status or future potential.

Bottom Fishing

When I started buying rental buildings, I was fixated on making absolutely sure that my investments would produce a positive cash flow. My goal was to find properties that offered the possibility of generating a positive cash flow, regardless of how paltry that cash flow might be: just don't run negative, I thought. Today, I still devote an inordinate amount of my time to buying properties that produce a positive cash flow, but I spend much more time than I once did making sure that acquisitions are made at substantial discounts so that the return on my capital is maximized during the hold period. I've purchased during market cycles when rents were declining, thereby causing cash flows to run negative. Acquiring properties at extraordinary discounts allows you to weather almost any sort of change in the market (downward pressure on rents or upward pressure on operating expenses—or both simultaneously) and still turn a profit. Buying low provides an extra layer of financial safety should market conditions change for the worse—and that cushion could mean the difference between positive and negative cash flow as well as between dismal and stellar returns.

"We would hang banners on buildings offering below-market lease rents," Marcel Arsenault, author of *How to Build a Real Estate Empire,* wrote. "But we were able to do this because our acquisition pricing allowed us that luxury." Mr. Arsenault always bought properties at significant discounts; thus, the debt service was low enough to enable him to continue generating positive cash flow, even during challenging economic times when he had to reduce rents to keep occupancy high. After all, no business can survive in the long run without generating a positive cash flow, and Marcel is fully aware of this . . . so he always aggressively underwrites each deal and buys properties at the "right" price.

Buying Low

Cash flow is based on the following basic formula:

Revenue
Less: Vacancy and collection costs
Less: Operating expenses
Equals: Net operating income (NOI)
Less: Debt service
Equals: Cash flow

Buying low and obtaining favorable financing will have a positive effect on debt service because the principal amount of the loan (and thus the monthly mortgage payment) will be less than it would have been if you had paid a higher price. Financing a smaller debt load (assuming the same terms) will always enhance cash flow. If you are able to increase a property's income while reducing its operating expenses, you will improve your property's net operating income. The most comprehensive way to enhance cash flow is to improve every element that influences cash flow. Increasing rents; reducing turnover, vacancies, and collection loss; buying low and obtaining favorable financing; making value-add improvements; and implementing aggressive management practices that reduce operating expenses will all work toward increasing cash flow. If an acute awareness of maximizing cash flow remains a constant in your investment strategy, I am confident that you'll be successful in this business.

I have friends (much savvier than I) who troll around banks and law firms searching for apartment buildings that they can obtain at 50 or 60 cents on the dollar. Although when I started, I was able to find and close more deals than they did in a given year, their properties generated superior returns because they spent more of their time and effort buying at the lowest possible price. These investors knew that significant and immediate gains are made at the closing table—when the price is right on a value-add deal, the returns can be staggering. I was satisfied with 15 percent returns until I realized that some of my good friends were realizing gains of 35 percent or more on their equity when they purchased low. After this realization, I was more determined to locate, negotiate, and close on properties that offered greater value. You, too, must be convinced that, although it may take more time and you may close fewer deals, doing this will be well worth the effort.

Negotiating a Better Price

Buying real estate at a steep discount requires a great deal of strategy and a well-designed plan. If the selling party believes that he is participating in fair negotiations, he will be more inclined to accept a discounted price. Because the seller may be a source of future properties, you never want to make him feel as if you have extracted all of the profit from the deal. Nevertheless, you should buy only good, moneymaking assets, regardless of whom you might upset with a low offer. To accomplish this feat, you should obtain answers to the following questions during the negotiation:

- What's the absolute lowest price that the seller or lender (in the case of a nonperforming loan) will accept?
- How much can I purchase the property for if I close quickly (assuming that you have the ability to do this)?
- What is the debt on the property? (How much does the seller owe to his lender(s) or what's the outstanding debt to the bank?)
- How much did the owner originally pay for the property?
- How much has the owner invested in property improvements while owning it?
- Why is the property being sold?
- Is the owner/lender motivated to sell?

Armed with this information, you should know the approximate price range that the owner will accept. As a last resort, I might be willing to show the owner how I arrived at my conservative and sometimes creative offer figure. My assumption is that, if I can logically justify my price, it will make the seller feel more comfortable that he isn't being taken advantage of in the negotiation—and that you aren't exacting too much of the upside from the deal.

Once you have agreed on a price and signed a sales contract, it's time to perform your due diligence on the apartment building. If in fact you find anything materially wrong with the property, you should return to the negotiating table with substantive reasons why you require a further discount. Use estimates from your general contractor indicating the cost to remedy a problem or make specific repairs. The more time you and the buyer spend negotiating a deal, the more committed he will be to seeing it closed and the less likely he will be to walk away from the negotiations. Plan your strategy wisely, and take your time. As the hours, days, and weeks pass, the owner will be increasingly less likely to reject a deal that he's invested so much of his time trying to close. However, if the buyer isn't at all motivated to sell, he might not accept your offer. Perhaps the seller has owned the property for the past 20 years and no longer has a mortgage. Without any debt, the property is probably generating a substantial cash flow, and the owner just isn't motivated to sell (especially at a discount to the current market value). In this case, you need to move on to your next opportunity. You cannot survive in the apartment building business if you waste your time dealing with owners who are not motivated to sell at the discounts you'll need.

Buying from Lenders

In down markets, opportunities abound (directly or indirectly) to buy from banks and other mortgage lenders because they are inundated with nonperforming loans. In such markets, lenders are more apt to sell a property for the outstanding balance of the mortgage or the current appraised value, or even to consider taking a loss, to remove these bad loans from their books. Banks are not in the business of being landlords and typically don't want to own real estate. They just want to finance the deals and earn interest on their loans. In fact, during an unprecedented seven-year run (from 2000 to 2006), lenders were underwriting loans for nearly every apartment condo conversion project under consideration. Just as in the dot.com days, when all you needed was a 25-year-old semiarticulate entrepreneur with a 35-page PowerPoint presentation to secure millions of dollars in financing for a new Internet start-up, during the past seven years, a similar presentation was all you needed in real estate. It seemed like anyone who could swing a hammer received financing for condo conversion projects.

Investing in Apartment Buildings

Because of the condo craze, apartment building values spiked during this period as the demand for these assets increased and the supply fell. According to Marcus & Millichap, approximately 315,000 apartments were converted to condos between 2003 and 2006. Lenders readily committed debt to these projects, often basing new loans on projections of future unit sales and not on apartment fundamentals such as the present net operating income and estimated cash flow on a rental basis. This strategy worked well for several years: banks made loans, pooled the debt, and sold it to the secondary market, making handsome fee-based profits. Now that the credit market has frozen and condos are no longer selling, converters are left with properties that they paid a premium for, but that do not generate enough rental income to enable the owners to meet their debt obligations. Converters bought and banks financed based on the assumption that all units would be renovated and the condos would be sold. Eventually, lenders will have been left with nonperforming loans (because of the enormous amount of debt that developers cannot pay) and real estate that they will be forced to liquidate. These problems are, in fact, tremendous opportunities for the savvy investor. However, to speak intelligently with a banker about such deals, you'll need to become more familiar with bankers' parlance: lis pendens, deed of trust, notice of default, deed in lieu of foreclosure, senior and mezzanine lenders, short sale, par value of the loan, deficiency note, foreclosure, and real estate owned are some of the terms used in the banking world.

Default

Typically, after 90 days of nonpayment, the owner of a property is declared to be in default. The loan officer notifies the mortgagor (the borrower in a mortgage) that he is at risk of losing his property to foreclosure, but he is usually granted a few months to pay the outstanding balance and "catch up" with the amount owed. The loan officer will place a red flag on this account before escalating the matter to the special assets division. Back in the early 1990s real estate bust, the department that was assigned the responsibility for managing nonperforming loans was called the workout team. These highly skilled individuals had three options after a property had been in default for more than three months:

1. Work out a repayment, refinancing, or restructuring of the deal with the mortgagor (borrower).
2. Begin the foreclosure procedure on the property.
3. Sell the note to another investor.

Today, these departments have the same function and options; however, they are referred as the special assets division. Don't let this name fool you. The assets are "special" only because they are in trouble!

Deed in Lieu of Foreclosure

A deed in lieu of foreclosure, or a "deed in lieu," is a way in which a mortgagor and mortgagee (the lender in a mortgage) can avoid the time-consuming and expensive foreclosure proceeding. The mortgagor (the borrower) conveys the interest in his property to the mortgagee (the lender) to satisfy a loan that is in default. That's a way of saying that, if the owner of the property can't pay his mortgage, he can give the bank legal ownership of the property and the bank will release him from his mortgage obligation. The borrower forfeits his equity in the property, and the bank ends up owning a property that it hopes to sell and recoup its investment.

The deed in lieu of foreclosure offers several advantages to both the borrower and the lender. The principal advantage to the borrower is that it immediately releases him from any guaranty associated with the defaulted loan. The borrower and the lender both avoid the public disclosure of a litigious proceeding—one that could tarnish both of their reputations. Also, a lender benefits because of the reduction in the time and cost associated with repossession by foreclosure, which can take up to one year, especially if the borrower files for bankruptcy. Generally, the lender will not pursue a deed in lieu of foreclosure if the outstanding balance of the loan exceeds the current fair market value of the property (the amount the bank could reasonably sell it for given existing market conditions). This is a general rule only; I have seen a multitude of variations on these types of transactions.

Senior versus Mezzanine Lenders

I once met with a developer who was converting a 360-unit Class A apartment complex near Fort Lauderdale. He had sold 55 percent of the units, but he couldn't sell more because of the housing meltdown. "We simply didn't see the crash coming," he commented. "It wasn't a gradual slow-down; the condo market simply fell off the cliff!" Unfortunately, he was just too late to the game. By the time we had scheduled our meeting, he had been in default for six months. His senior lender had offered him a six-month extension; however, the mezzanine lender refused to provide any extensions and began to foreclose, as it wanted to use its equity warrants to secure control of the property. The developer filed for bankruptcy to keep the mezzanine lender at bay in hopes of delaying long enough to find a solution to his dilemma—a $200,000 monthly burn rate!

Note: Mezzanine debt is capital that is in the "middle," between senior loans and equity. Mezzanine debt ranks junior to bank loans and often carries equity warrants that allow the mezzanine lender to become the operator of the property in the event of a default.

Senior loans generally receive the highest priority for repayment of principal and payment of interest. In a default situation, senior loans usually are repaid first, before other classes of subordinated or junior debt (second or mezzanine loans). Senior loans often are used for acquisitions, recapitalizations, and restructurings and cover the majority of the purchase price of a property. In many instances, a senior lender will finance up to 80 percent of the purchase price. For example, if a property costs $1 million, senior financing might provide $800,000; the difference (or $200,000) could come from the buyer's savings, the buyer's friends and family, a mezzanine line, a secondary loan, or in some instances a combination of these.

Mezzanine loans are often used by developers to secure additional financing for development projects such as the renovation of an apartment complex for conversion. Mezzanine or "mezz" loans (as they are often referred to) are basically loan instruments that give the lender the right to convert its debt to an equity (ownership) interest in the property if the loan is not paid back in a timely way. Mezzanine lenders secure their loans by using the borrower's equity interest in the building as collateral. If a borrower defaults on his loan, the mezzanine provider can become the property's new owner. In case of default, this conversion of debt to equity reduces the mezz lender's risk, for its loan is subordinate (in second place) to debt provided by senior lenders such as banks and other traditional lenders. That said, because mezz loans are inherently riskier forms of debt, they command interest rates that are sometimes double or triple those of senior loans.

Short Sale

In a short sale, the purchase price is insufficient to cover the amount necessary to pay off all liens and/or encumbrances (first and second mortgages, prepayment penalties, and so on) secured by the property and the expenses associated with the sale. A short sale usually occurs when a property is in default and the foreclosure has yet to take place. The lender will opt for a short sale if it believes that doing so will result in a smaller loss than going through a foreclosing procedure. For a short sale to work, the lender must agree to accept a discounted payoff from a buyer. In other words, the lender must be willing to receive less money (from the sale of the property) than it is actually owed in exchange for releasing the "short seller" from his obligation to pay the loan.

Foreclosure

If the owner and/or the lender fails to secure a short sale and the owner hasn't made a mortgage payment in about 120 days after receiving the first late payment notice (this obviously varies from bank to bank), the lender typically will begin the foreclosure process to obtain possession of the property.

A foreclosure is a legal proceeding in which the mortgagee (usually a bank or other financial institution) repossesses a property after a borrower fails to meet his contractual mortgage obligation. In other words, the borrower is delinquent on his payments, and the lien holder (the lender) attempts to receive legal title to the property. In some instances, when a mortgagor defaults, a court can demand that he pay the mortgage within a specified time. If the mortgagor doesn't do so, the lender can eventually gain legal title to the property and dispose of the asset if it chooses.

Some banks prefer to avoid foreclosure because of the expense and time (sometimes up to one full year) required for this process. Also, banks prefer not to make public the status of their nonperforming loans, because this can bring unwanted attention by the media and scrutiny by the FDIC (a government agency that regulates all banks that are members of the Federal Reserve System).

Real Estate Owned

Real estate owned, or REO, is essentially property owned by a lender after the borrower defaults on his loan and the lender forecloses on the property.

REOs are becoming more and more common these days (as they were in the early 1970s and 1990s) because of the recession, the housing meltdown, the subprime debacle, readjusting mortgage loans, inflation/ stagflation, and the credit crunch. A very large percentage of the assets for sale at REO auctions during troubled times have negative equity (they are worth less than the existing debt), and therefore banks find it challenging to liquidate their REO inventory.

Once a property becomes part of a lender's REO inventory, the lender attempts to sell the property (usually at a loss) through an auction or a more traditional channel such as a Realtor. To make the property more marketable, the lender might even consider making renovations and other improvements and removing any outstanding liens. The most common types of liens are tax and mechanic's liens. Tax liens are made when the owner doesn't pay his property taxes. Mechanic's liens are filed when vendors provide services at the property but aren't compensated for the improvements made, so they file a lien to recoup their expenses.

Because banks aren't in the business of owning real estate, they are motivated to remove these bad loans from their books. They might accept a loss on these loans, but they are not eager to lose money, so they might take their time and, at least initially, refuse to sell at a discount. If the FDIC is overseeing the lender's activities, it's even more difficult for the lender to accept significant discounts. At the beginning of a down cycle, lenders are less motivated to discount loans; however, as the market worsens and lenders become inundated with properties, they begin to sell at greater and greater discounts. This occurred in 1989 with great frequency, and this current cycle should be no different.

To be exposed to these opportunities, you must befriend loan officers, REO personnel, and special asset managers. You must know which banks made loans to investors in multifamily assets and who within each bank is responsible for the disposition of these assets. Once you have access to these deals, you'll be able to work directly with the lender to acquire properties at potentially steep discounts. Also, you might be able to work out a deal with a bank if the owner is willing to introduce you to his loan officer and negotiate a favorable sale before it is escalated to special assets, assuming that the borrower is in trouble and can no longer meet his financial obligations.

I have a friend in Chicago who partnered with a company that specializes in the boarding up of foreclosed properties. This company is the first to learn of a troubled property because it secures the exterior of abandoned buildings until the bank can evaluate the property. My friend makes offers on these properties before any Realtor or investor gets the chance to buy them in the open market. There are numerous ways in which you can buy discounted properties; however, you must continue to work diligently to establish a network that provides you with these opportunistic buying opportunities.

In fact, Freddie Mac has created a Web site to sell some of its troubled properties:

Web site: www.homesteps.com.

REO opportunities are difficult to finance through conventional sources. They often require the investor to place a large portion of the purchase price, if not 100 percent, down. Lenders want quick, easy closings with no mortgage contingencies. Higher interest rates, renovation costs, and down payment requirements can make a seemingly good deal an extremely bad one, so do your homework and know what you're getting into before the closing.

Chapter Summary

- Spend considerably more time and effort searching for properties that you can buy at a discount.
- Buying low allows you to be more competitive with rents during the lean years and provides a basis from which you are able to maximize cash flow during periods of high growth.
- Create your own pro forma statements and don't rely on the owner's financial projections.
- An income-producing property's value must be based primarily on its current net operating income (assuming future operating expenses—if anticipated to increase—are factored into the equation).
- Negotiate the best deal every time you buy.
- Buy only from motivated sellers.
- Banks are not in the real estate investing business. They will often sell REOs and nonperforming loans at steep discounts.

7

Due Diligence

Nothing will ever be attempted if all possible objections must be first overcome.

—SAMUEL JOHNSON

What You're About to Learn

- What due diligence is and why it's so important
- How to evaluate the competition
- Pro forma income statements
- Net operating income
- Cash-on-cash return
- Cap rate analysis
- Debt service coverage ratio

There are always a million "what ifs" when performing the due diligence on any real estate deal. All too often, risk-averse investors conjure up a multitude of reasons (unfounded as they may be) and convince themselves not to proceed with a given transaction. These individuals find it difficult to "pull the trigger" on any project, regardless of its potential.

Defined: In investment parlance, "pulling the trigger" refers to the ability to close. This phrase is often used with a negative connotation to refer to someone who considers many deals but rarely buys any of them.

Real estate investors certainly must acknowledge the risks associated with purchasing income-producing properties; however, they also must devise a sound plan for addressing and minimizing those risks, or they will never buy anything. In fact, a good friend of mine talked himself out of countless opportunities and never invested in apartment buildings, even though he was eager and seemingly ready—and asked me on numerous occasions to include him on future projects.

A few years ago, a lawyer presented me with a very good opportunity on a foreclosed apartment building. It was well located, but it was vacant and required a complete renovation. I showed this property to this friend and gave him the opportunity to become my partner on the project. After touring the apartment building, he was excited to participate in his first deal, but asked for more time to conduct his own due diligence. His general contractor, property inspector, banker, broker, accountant, and attorney toured the building, and each of them responded with positive feedback. Even though his entire investment team encouraged him to proceed, he opted out of the deal at the last minute. Although I respected his opinion, I realized that his risk profile was not well suited for real estate.

Sometimes it takes a leap of faith to make such a large investment. Often you can overanalyze a deal to the point where you convince yourself that a wonderful opportunity is really a money-losing proposition. Paralysis by analysis sets in, and your visceral instincts are replaced with less accurate but colorful pie charts and statistics that complicate the decision-making process. Some individuals analyze deals so extensively that they always seem to find insurmountable challenges at every turn. By contrast, most successful real estate investors are creative entrepreneurs who are willing to assume a certain amount of risk for a commensurate amount of reward. "The more 'hair' on the deal the better," they say, because they'll benefit from a significant discount to the purchase price while still being able to manage any problems that may arise—problems that make it impossible for most other investors to see the forest for the trees.

Defined: Hair is a term used to describe a financial transaction or investment that offers less than ideal circumstances; it is risky or has complications. I suspect the hair makes it ugly. Fortunately, beauty is in the eye of the beholder.

Understanding Due Diligence

Perfect deals with absolutely no associated risk just *do not* exist, so don't waste your time searching for them. In fact, the more challenges there are associated with a project, the more reward one typically can derive from one's efforts. Don't be paralyzed by an inability to take action. Make a calculated decision to invest (or not) based on your ability to achieve the rate of return necessary given the amount of risk assumed. We all make mistakes in this business, but if you do your homework and follow the advice provided in this book, you'll do just fine.

Due diligence requires the buyer to verify *everything* before proceeding to the closing table. In addition to the physical condition of the property, there are a multitude of intangibles that must be considered when you are evaluating an apartment building for acquisition. Every document (especially the financials) related to an asset's historical operation should be examined, and you must confirm that everything you have been told about the property is accurate. The ability to conduct a thorough due diligence is a critical component of your success as a real estate investor. Also, verifying your own assumptions regarding the property's future performance (after the closing) is paramount. Most important, the due diligence period gives the buyer time to learn as much as possible about the asset before taking ownership (to avoid any costly surprises), so take your time and be thorough.

> *Defined: Due diligence* is an investigation of a potential investment that is conducted before making the actual purchase. Due diligence is used to confirm all the assumptions made about a property. A decision to purchase an asset is usually dependent on the findings from a thorough due diligence analysis. This includes reviewing all financial records, third-party reports, historical data, and anything else deemed relevant to the sale.

In this chapter, you will learn, for example, why a property may be worth only $700,000 even if the owner is demanding $1 million for it. Once you're able to calculate a property's value based on its current performance and future potential, making offers with confidence becomes much easier. Also, knowing how much you're able to offer will save you time by allowing you to avoid acquisition targets in which the owner has unrealistic expectations. It's far better to make an offer, receive an unrealistic counteroffer (or none at all), and quickly decide to move on if the seller isn't willing to consider what you're able to pay. I've spent months explaining to sellers why my offer price was reasonable—why, for example, $700,000 rather than $1 million made sense—only to realize that they were not going to accept my number. It's always better to determine sooner rather than later that a deal is not going to materialize. That way, you can concentrate your valuable time and energy on the next opportunity.

> *Lesson learned:* On numerous occasions, I've made what were in my opinion reasonable offers, but the seller decided not to make a counteroffer or to reduce his asking price. However, after spending months in fruitless attempts to sell their property, owners (including lenders of foreclosed properties) can suddenly become significantly more motivated to sell. In many instances, sellers have returned to the negotiating table (albeit a few months later) inquiring about my continued interest in their properties. Always be patient, and never chase deals that don't make financial sense.

Is a price of $2.5 million for a 24-unit apartment complex a great deal, a good deal, or an overpriced, money-losing problem? You won't know the answer to this critical question unless you fully understand how to evaluate such properties. Becoming an astute analyst who knows how to use financial models for evaluating multifamily apartment buildings will help you make a lot of money. Please keep that in mind as you peruse the rest of this chapter.

Property Data

The information provided by the owner includes current rental rates, concessions, lease information, vendor contracts, historical expenditures, management reports, operating expenses, and other such data. The verification of all this information is part of your fiduciary responsibility to your investors (assuming that you have them) and should not be taken lightly. After all, the final conclusion made as a result of the due diligence will be either to buy or not to buy. Acquiring a property based on false or misleading data could result in lower returns or even the loss of your equity. Neglecting to perform a rigorous due diligence analysis on a prospective new acquisition target could cause you to overpay for a property.

The less familiar you are with an area, the more time you'll need to ensure the validity of the information being given to you. That's precisely why staying within your farm area is so critical. Your analysis is likely to be more accurate if you intimately know the area where you are buying.

For example, after touring a property in your farm area, you should immediately know the market rent for each of the units. Moreover, you'll know how quickly vacancies can be filled, whether or not concessions must be offered, and what the stabilized occupancy rate for the property is likely to be. You'll also know how much all the operating expenses (such as taxes, insurance, maintenance, electricity, sewer/water, and garbage disposal) should be. Being familiar with the area will allow you to make fairly quick decisions regarding the accuracy of the data provided.

If you are less familiar with an area, you'll need to work a bit harder to complete your due diligence. Institutional investors are able to acquire properties throughout the country because they have the resources needed to ensure their success, but as previously mentioned, I recommend that you stay close to home if you are a less seasoned entrepreneur or the principal of a small investment group.

> *Lesson learned:* I once acquired a property outside my farm area and clearly didn't know as much as I should have regarding the existing tenants, the area, market rents, vacancy rates, the competition, crime, and other such factors. In other words, I did not perform a thorough due diligence but made the investment anyway. I learned a lesson in humility with that property. Today, I consider such experiences "school fees" in my already very expensive real estate education.

Property Inspection

Institutional investors can easily spend $10,000 to $20,000 on a third-party inspection of a property consisting of a couple of hundred units. Although inspections of smaller properties will cost less but probably won't be as extensive, you still can use some of the same methods employed by large institutions, private equity firms, and REITs when evaluating smaller projects.

A property condition assessment (PCA) and an environmental site assessment (ESA) report must be prepared for any new property under consideration. In fact, many lending institutions, including Fannie Mae and Freddie Mac, require these reports

The PCA Report

The PCA report contains information about the structure of a property and all of its components—information that is critical to evaluating a property.

A standard report should comply with the industry standards established by the American Society for Testing and Materials (ASTM) and should consider the following:

Due Diligence

Site	Basements	Exterior
Foundation	Fencing/gates	Interior
Structure	Electrical	Roofs
HVAC	Plumbing	Parking area
Safety and compliance	Current deficiencies	Deferred maintenance

Note: ASTM was formed more than 100 years ago. It is one of the largest organizations in the world that develops and formulates standards.

Of the areas that should be inspected, the three "big ticket" items are given first.

Roof Inspection

The age of the roof(s) is determined, and its condition, lifespan, and cost of replacement are given.

Structural and Foundation Inspection

An assessment of the foundation and an evaluation of its soundness are provided.

HVAC Inspection

The heating, ventilation, and air conditioning systems and air handlers are assessed.

Interior Inspection

If you're working on a large apartment complex, with several hundred units spread over multiple buildings, the inspector will probably enter less than 30 percent of the units, unless instructed otherwise, and will make an assessment based on his findings in those units. If, for example, an evaluation of a 300-unit complex were being conducted, 30 to 90 units would be assessed and examined thoroughly. You can pay an additional fee to have the inspection company enter all of the units (I recommend doing so). If you're buying a small multifamily property (two to four units), the inspector will enter every apartment, tour the basement (if applicable), and inspect the roof, common areas, and the grounds.

During the interior inspection, the electrical systems, plumbing (checking for leaks), ceiling (checking for any water damage), cleanliness of units, preexisting or potential safety hazards, and security of windows and doors are all evaluated.

Finally, a table of capital reserve requirements should be included at the end of the report. This information will indicate how much you'll need to invest over the next five to ten years to make necessary improvements or repairs to the property. Capital improvements are any permanent structural improvement or restoration that will either increase the property's useful life or enhance its overall value.

Ideally, the property inspector will be experienced in his line of work. Be sure to request a veteran inspector who has been with the company for many years. If you conclude that the inspector assigned to your property is wet behind the ears (right out of college or trade school) and has limited experience, be concerned. You sometimes get what you ask for (or don't ask for) in life.

If you are going to work with a specific property management company or if you have already chosen your on-site property manager, that company or manager should be willing to enter every unit (above and beyond the units that the inspection company already evaluated) and provide you with their own detailed summary report, since you are going to offer them the job of managing the building or apartment complex. Typically, your manager will conduct this inspection for a nominal charge, or perhaps at no expense to the buyer. After all, he'll need to know the condition of the property and would unlikely be able to sign off on the first year's proposed budget until he has familiarized himself with the condition of the property.

During the due diligence period, I always ask the property manager to review my operating statement and suggest modifications. If he concludes that it's not accurate or achievable, we'll consider making adjustments. The interests of the property manager and the buyer should always be aligned, because a budget will be drafted and agreed to by *both* parties before the closing. If the manager fails to achieve the goals outlined (and agreed to), he will be held accountable. Because of this, the manager is encouraged to spend as much time as possible getting familiar with a

Due Diligence

property so that he can prepare an operating budget that is achievable. Also, because the manager's compensation is based on the property's performance, his pay will suffer if the stated goals are not met.

In Figure 7.1, you'll find a unit inspection report that one of my property managers drafted for our internal use. This document is useful

Due Diligence Report

Address: _____   Condition

Unit #: _____

	Good	Average	Poor
Air Conditioner			
Bathroom Cabinets			
Bedroom 1			
Bedroom 2			
Bedroom 3			
Ceiling			
Closets			
Dishwasher			
Doors			
Drapes/Blinds			
Faucets			
Garbage Disposal			
Heater			
Kitchen Cabinets			
Kitchen Counters			
Paint			
Refrigerator			
Shower Door/Curtain Rod			
Sinks			
Stove			
Toilet			
Tub/Shower			
Vanity			
Water Heater			
Windows			

Tenant

Misc. Notes

Figure 7.1 Unit Inspection Report

during the property inspection period, as I always request that one form be completed for every unit prior to closing. It provides us with a status report for every unit and gives us an idea of the amount of work that will be required to ensure that each unit meets our minimum standards of quality.

Contractor Inspection

A general contractor's inspection report is required only when a property needs extensive work. Often, entire units or common areas and grounds must be upgraded to provide a safe living environment for the tenants. A general contractor typically will provide a detailed report with estimates to make the requisite improvements or structural repairs to the property.

The ESA Report

The Phase I ESA report identifies potential or existing environmental contamination liabilities. Such an analysis will consider the condition of the property and the underlying land from an environmental perspective. This examination includes investigating potential soil contamination, groundwater quality, and surface water quality; identification of materials possibly containing asbestos; inventory of hazardous substances stored or used on site, assessment of mold and mildew, checking for the existence of lead in the paint or in the drinking water, and evaluation of radon readings at the property.

A determination is made as to whether the property was built on a dump site or contaminated land. If a site is considered contaminated, a Phase II ESA is recommended and should be conducted. It contains a more detailed investigation, including actual collection of physical samples from the property and chemical analyses of those samples. The ESA report should comply with the industry standards established by ASTM and the U.S. Environmental Protection Agency.

Once, while conducting the due diligence of a 200-unit apartment complex in West Palm Beach, Florida, I worked with an inspection company that submitted aerial photos dating all the way back to 1930. We wanted to make sure that the site hadn't been used as an orchard (which is common in southern Florida). On land used for the harvesting of fruits and vegetables, historically large quantities of pesticides were employed to protect the vegetation, plants, and trees. Pesticides are dangerous chemicals that can penetrate the soil and cause a great deal of contamination. Be careful that you're not buying a property that was built where an industrial site, gas station, or orchard had been decades ago.

Note: Environmental Data Resources Corp. is the leading provider of environmental information. In addition to providing historical aerial photos of any given location, it offers the largest and most accurate database of environmental and historical land use information in the world.

Web site: www.edrnet.com.

The inspection report also will estimate the costs of any major capital expenditures required. These findings may alter your pro forma analysis, so take them into consideration. You always can renegotiate the price of the property if the remedies are exorbitant.

A typical ESA report should include the following:

Asbestos	Lead in the drinking water
Air quality	Mold
Radon	Hazardous material on site
Lead-based paint	Ground soil
Recommendation for Phase II reporting	

Why Be Concerned about Environmental Hazards?

Digesting *lead* by eating tainted paint chips or drinking polluted drinking water is known to cause mental retardation, liver problems, and serious learning disabilities. Properties built before 1978 (the last year manufacturers were allowed to use lead in their paint) are likely to contain high concentrations of lead on the premises unless the property was completely renovated or the lead paint was encapsulated. Until 1978, lead paint often was used on both the interiors and the exteriors of homes throughout the country. The U.S. Department of Housing and Urban Development (HUD) estimates that approximately 38 million homes in the United States still contain some lead paint. Lead paint that is intact (not peeling or chipping) is not an immediate concern, but lead paint that is deteriorating does pose a hazard, so remediation must be carried out if children under six years of age reside on the property.

Radon is a known carcinogen and the second-leading cause of lung cancer after smoking. Radon is an odorless gas formed in soil, rock, and water. It exists in the ground and can seep into an apartment building through cracks and holes in the foundation. It can also enter through the well water. To prevent high levels of radon, adequate ventilation is required, and cracks in the property's foundation must be sealed.

Asbestos was the substance most commonly used to insulate buildings before 1972. However, scientists have found that breathing asbestos fibers can result in several diseases, including lung cancer. Asbestos can be found in ceiling tiles, flooring, and around pipes. It becomes a danger only when it is disturbed, causing the fibers to get into the air (as opposed to settling on a surface) and thus endangering the air you breathe. The more exposure one has to inhaling these dangerous asbestos fibers, the greater the likelihood of contracting serious lung diseases.

> *Note:* If you're considering the purchase of a property and you notice any 9- by 9-inch tiles on the floor, there's a good chance that they contain asbestos. At about the same time that it was realized that asbestos was dangerous to our health, 9- by 9-inch tiles became outdated and were replaced with more fashionable 12- by 12-inch tiles.

Water quality is important to all of your tenants. ESAs should include the testing of drinking water to determine whether there are dangerous concentrations of lead, copper, particulates (sediment), or any bacteria. These contaminants can be dangerous for your residents' health. The water should be safe to drink and acceptable for all other household uses.

Inspection Companies

Here is a short list of national companies that provide ESA and PCA reporting:

ATC Associates: www.atcassociates.com

Criterium Engineers: www.criterium-commercial.com

LM Consultants: www.lmconsultants.com

ENSR: www.ensr.aecom.com

Terracon: www.terracon.com

Most institutional investors have a fiduciary responsibility to obtain these reports. If you invest in smaller properties, you still want to have a professional inspection conducted to avoid buying someone else's problem. If, for example, you're considering a small apartment building, then, at a minimum, a licensed company that specializes in this line of work should complete a thorough inspection of the property. Its experts will enter every unit and evaluate the exterior of the property, HVAC, roof, foundation, and electrical and plumbing systems. A certified report will be given to you after the inspection, detailing all of the inspectors' findings. It will highlight any areas of concern that need to be addressed. Some firms will make specific recommendations and provide estimates for the repairs. The inspection report gives you a professional opinion about the apartment building that you're about to buy.

Qualitative Due Diligence

As mentioned earlier in this chapter, a qualitative analysis is based more on personal opinion than on measurable data points. The following is a list of items that I ascertain before buying any property:

The seller:

Property name.

Property address.

Investing in Apartment Buildings

Owner's name or entity.

When did the current owner acquire the property?

The asking price of the property.

What was the current owner's purchase price for the property?

How much has the owner invested in the property since the acquisition date?

What's the total amount of debt owed on the property?

Which bank(s) is (are) holding the debt?

How long has the property been on the market?

Is the property in default or foreclosure?

The tenants:

How many tenants receive housing assistance?

Are tenants relatively cooperative and friendly?

Are there any tenant issues (drug sales, nonpayment, gangs, cleanliness, noise)?

Number of annual leases versus TAW (tenant at will) breakdown.

Are tenants historically long term or short term?

Are pets allowed?

The location:

Is it a commercial or strictly a residential area?

Describe properties adjacent to the subject property.

What type of street is this property on: one way, dead end, double or single yellow line?

Proximity to schools.

Proximity to public transportation.

Proximity to hospitals.

Due Diligence

Aerial maps.

Pictures of the property and the surrounding area (present and past).

The building (physical):

Mix of units

Number of buildings

Land size

Number of floors

Framing

Parking

Concern for lead

Elevators

Condition of roof

Age of roof

Condition of air handlers/condensers

Condition of stairwells

Electrical amps and condition of systems—copper or
  aluminum wiring

Electrical breakers or fuses

Individually metered for water and electricity

Power outages because of inadequate electrical systems

Age/condition of hot water heaters

Foundation

Window conditions

Door conditions

Washers/dryers

Refrigerators

Asbestos

Mold

Insects/rodents/termites

Miscellaneous:

Have there been any insurance claims during the past five years?

Is there an on-site manager and maintenance staff?

Are contractual agreements for trash removal, laundry, and landscaping in place?

Zoning issues (illegal units, illegal use)

Is parking or storage a separate charge?

Is laundry coin- or card-operated? Is there a service contract?

Is the owner willing to provide certified copies of income and expenses?

Proof of all rental deposits for the past month.

One-year operating statement, certified (signed by the owners).

Nearby apartment complexes—vacancy rates, rents, comparable units, and other such information.

Major employers in the area.

Speak to and obtain feedback from:

Local police: obtain the number of call-outs and a crime report for the past five years.

Postal delivery carrier.

Local property managers.

Nearby property owners (tour similar properties and verify the rents and the condition of the units).

Tenants.

The property manager.

The on-site maintenance crew.

Vendors.

This is my personal qualitative due diligence list. Depending on your area and your specific concerns, you may add additional items to or remove some from this list. The most important element of this process is to create your own comprehensive list of questions to ask in order to analyze a property—and to be diligent in making sure that you have all the facts before the closing.

Online Research

Evaluating a property's location and appeal to prospective tenants will help you determine whether you'll have difficulty filling vacancies. One way to gauge the market quickly in terms of tenant demand for any rental property is to post an ad on Craigslist. Take a few photos of the interior and exterior of the building. Place these photos on www.craiglist .org with a short description of the unit available, the rent asked, and a description of the amenities. Within a few days, you should receive several phone calls or e-mails. Take the opportunity to speak with these prospective tenants. The response (or lack thereof) will enable you to better gauge the current market conditions for the property. This is a simple and nonscientific test of the market conditions and demand for the units you might be attempting to lease should you decide to purchase the property. The results are provided free of charge, and the feedback is almost immediate. Within a few hours or days, you'll know whether there's significant, moderate, or lower than expected demand because Craigslist is extremely effective in most communities. (By the way, the names of all prospective tenants should be forwarded to the current owner or property manager for immediate consideration.)

You also should visit one of the tenant rating sites. Renters use these Web sites to provide feedback (likes and dislikes) regarding the rental communities in which they have lived. Unfortunately, some ratings are posted by the property manager or the owner (who have a vested interest in posting positive reviews) rather than by tenants, so be forewarned.

The following are comments from two "tenants" with differing opinions who lived at the same apartment building in Boston:

Tenant 1:
What a great location, nice units, and a friendly staff. Incredible location; the pool deck on the mezzanine level is an oasis in the city and extremely relaxing.

Rating: 5 out of 5

Tenant 2:
This is the biggest dump in Boston. Dirt ground into the hall floors, horrid smells everywhere, pool out of use, annoying doorman.

Rating: 1 out of 5

Apartment Ratings is one of the largest online rental housing communities, with more than 600,000 ratings and reviews of apartments nationwide.

Web sites: Apartment rating firms:

http://www.apartmentratings.com
http://www.apartmentreviews.net

The Competition

To gain competitive information on nearby apartment complexes, I conduct reconnaissance missions within a five-mile radius of the subject property. You can introduce yourself to the property manager as a prospective buyer of a nearby apartment building who is in need of information. If you don't feel confident that being so forthright will allow you to extract the information you are seeking, try introducing yourself as a local business owner who provides housing to its key employees. Such an introduction tends to disarm the manager and allows him to feel more comfortable about sharing proprietary information such as rents, concessions, current vacancy rate, historical vacancy rates, the mix of units, market conditions, issues with crime, amenities offered, and so on. Also, I always inquire about the manager's opinion of the property I am considering buying. I've conducted these reconnaissance missions numerous times for many years and have managed to obtain extremely valuable information about the competition while learning a lot about the property I was evaluating.

Individuals Who Are Knowledgeable about the Property

Postal Carrier

Speak with the postal delivery agent. After all, he delivers mail to the property every day. He probably speaks with tenants, is aware of potential or existing problems, and is familiar with the property. I'm always surprised just how much these carriers know.

Tenants

Would you buy a restaurant without speaking to the patrons? There are no laws (as far as I know) that prohibit you from speaking with the current tenants. After all, they will be your future customers, and you need to know what they think.

During the due diligence period, be sure to visit the property in the evening and notice the number of cars in the parking lot. Then go there in the middle of the day to see whether the majority of the cars are still there. This seemingly insignificant detail provides an indication as to whether the tenant base is employed during the day. Although some tenants might work the night shift, if there are a lot of cars in the lot during the day, most of them probably don't work at all. In general, people with jobs (and stay-at-home moms) tend to be able to pay rent, are more responsible renters, and make better tenants.

On-Site Property Manager

If the on-site manager is aware of the pending sale, you should have a frank discussion with him to learn his views about the property. Unless he has been instructed to hide the truth from prospective buyers, the manager should be able to offer a wealth of information and should know more than anyone else about the asset's day-to-day operations. Inquire about his interest in continuing to work at the property, if you're at all interested in retaining his services. If he wants to keep his job, he will be more receptive and responsive to your questions. On-site managers should be acutely aware of any difficulties, including vacancies, tenant problems, deferred maintenance, and crime.

During the due diligence period, I always ask both the current manager and my own manager for a list of the top 10 things that each would change at the property to enhance the net operating income (NOI). I also ask both of them to prepare a capital budget to pay for these changes. Comparing the two reports is always quite illuminating. This information, if deemed accurate, is then used to update my pro forma for the property.

Maintenance Staff

Maintenance personnel spend a lot of time at the property. They speak with the tenants, make all the repairs, and know how much work is required to maintain the property. You should be able to learn about any deferred maintenance issues from these individuals.

Police Call-Out Reports

When buying a property, you should always obtain a call-out report from the local police department. This report will indicate each time the police were called to the property. Issues range from tenants complaining about their neighbor's music to homicides and everything in between. The sergeant assigned to the area should be able to provide information regarding your particular property.

The Shadow Effect

The shadow effect is created when single-family homes and condos that haven't been sold by their developers are returned to the market as rentals, creating an oversupply of product and reducing the overall demand for rental housing. Be careful if you find yourself in one of the following markets because they have experienced an abundance of new construction during the past few years: Orlando, Palm Beach, Fort Lauderdale, Miami, Houston, Las Vegas, San Diego, and Phoenix. The markets in these areas have weakened as a "shadow inventory" of unsold condo units is competing for tenants. Faced with an abundance of units for sale, many developers have reverted their properties to rental communities (this is called "condo reversion"). New condo units that did not sell are now back on the market as rentals and are competing with rental units that probably have fewer amenities and lack the upgrades that were made to condo-ready units.

When this excess inventory returns to the market as rentals, the increased supply will cast a shadow over the existing rental supply and will negatively affect existing multifamily properties. Real Capital Analytics estimates that between 2004 and 2006, 331,000 apartments were sold to condo converters nationwide, but 31,500 of those units have already been reverted to rentals. According to data researcher Reis Inc:

- The vacancy rate in Palm Beach County alone has risen by 280 basis points in the past year, to 7 percent.
- Orlando's vacancy rate increased by 140 basis points, to 6.2 percent, during the past year.

That's not to say that these areas are doomed forever. More and more people are moving to the Sun Belt each year, and job creation, immigration, and unemployment continue to improve, so properties in these areas should ultimately produce a good return for investors who have long-term strategies.

Alternatively, some of the healthiest rental markets continue to be New York City, Seattle, San Francisco, Oakland, and Orange County, California. These areas benefit from strong fundamentals such as rent growth and job formation and are less affected by the shadow inventory caused by new condo developments.

Rental Demand

On a more macroeconomic level, at the time of my book's publication, the *National Real Estate Investor* reported that the apartment vacancy rate was approximately 5.8 percent nationwide, and that rental income growth was outpacing inflation (essentially, rents were increasing faster than operating expenses). Investors should achieve above-average returns because these conditions should continue to improve as a result of the subprime market headaches (more owners losing their homes and becoming renters), an increase in the rental base from echo boomers who are just now entering their thirties, and increased demand from immigration that should add another 12 million potential renters to the market during the next seven years.

According to the *New York Times*, "Shifting demographics augur well for the big landlords: new households [will be created] as a result of a rising number of immigrants and young adults leaving the family fold, and aging baby boomers looking to downsize . . . all these factors seem favorable for landlords."

If you can buy value-add projects that have the potential to yield above-average returns and hire competent property managers, you'll have a good chance of succeeding. Just do your homework, perform a thorough due diligence, and manage the property well.

Quantitative (Financial) Due Diligence

Careful financial analysis is required for every single property you consider purchasing. In addition to the qualitative (more subjective) review, the underlying numbers behind a property are essential to determining what it is worth. Fully understanding these concepts places you at a distinct advantage in knowing how much you are willing to pay for a property. It stands to reason that if you don't know how to calculate the value of a property, you may overpay for it and, in the process, set yourself up for failure. The rest of this chapter is dedicated to making sure that this doesn't happen.

As mentioned, there are so many variables and assumptions involved in the analysis of a property that it's almost impossible to create a pro forma statement that is 100 percent accurate. However, if you're using the mathematical models outlined in this book, the margin of error should be minimal.

Due Diligence Materials to Request

Here are the materials you should request:

- Operating statements for the past two years
- Real estate tax bills for the past three years

- Copies of all current service contracts in force
- Current rent roll (for the past month)
- Copies of all rental income depository bank statements for the past 12 months
- Current vacancy rate and vacancy rate by month for the past three years
- Summary of capital repairs made by the owner since purchase
- Current year's operating budget
- Copies of any environmental reports
- All utility bills for the past two years
- Copies of any insurance loss claims for the past five years
- Copies of all current leases
- Copy of the most recent rental competition market analysis
- Listing of any pending litigation
- Property survey

Financial Analysis

There are three basic methods used to determine the value of any real estate asset:

1. Sales comparison approach
2. Replacement cost approach
3. Income approach

The sales comparison approach is most often used when determining the value of a single-family home or condominium. The replacement cost approach typically is used with special-purpose or unique properties such as churches, public buildings (e.g., fire stations), or schools. These properties are unique and don't necessarily have any comparable sales to reference. Finally, the income approach is used to determine the value of income-producing properties such as apartment buildings. If you want to buy and sell residential multifamily properties, you must become intimately familiar with the income approach.

The income approach uses a property's NOI to determine its value. Using the NOI and an acceptable market capitalization rate, you can determine the value (or price) using the following formula:

$$\text{Price} = \frac{\text{NOI}}{\text{Cap rate}}$$

Income Approach

Net operating income is calculated in the following way:

Gross scheduled (or potential) income (GSI)
Less: Vacancy and collection loss (V&C)
Equals: Net rental income
Plus: Other income (laundry, parking, storage, and so on)
Equals: Effective gross income (EGI)
Less: Operating expenses (OE)
Equals: Net operating income (NOI)
(All numbers are annualized.)

First, determine the annual gross scheduled income for the property. This involves calculating the amount of rent that all the units in the property generate each month and multiplying it by 12 (number of months in the year) to obtain the annual gross (potential) scheduled rental income. GSI assumes that 100 percent of the units are occupied.

Second, calculate the net rental income for the property by reducing the GSI by a vacancy allowance and a collection/concession amount. The vacancy allowance is determined by current market rental conditions for the class and location of the property under consideration. A collection loss is rent that you are unable to collect from tenants because of nonpayments; concessions are enticements (e.g., a free month's rent) given to prospective tenants to encourage them to sign a lease.

Defined: Vacancy rate is the percent of physically unoccupied units throughout the apartment complex. It's calculated by dividing the number of vacant units by the total number of units in the apartment building or complex.

Third, determine the EGI by adding to the net rental income any other income the property generates that is not rent-based (sometimes referred to as ancillary income). This includes fees from parking, laundry, storage, valet trash, satellite TV, vending machines, and so on.

Fourth, operating expenses such as water, common electricity, maintenance, property management, taxes, and so forth are deducted from the effective gross income to calculate the annual net operating income for the property.

The following is an example for further illustration:

Gross scheduled income	$50,000
Less: Vacancy and collection amount	$5,000
Equals: Net rental income	$45,000
Plus: Other income	$2,000
Equals: Effective gross income	$47,000
Less: Operating expenses	$20,000
Equals: Net operating income	$27,000

Cap Rate

Once the net operating income has been determined, a capitalization rate is calculated for the property using this formula:

$$\text{Cap rate} = \frac{\text{Net operating income}}{\text{Purchase price}}$$

One way to arrive at a cap rate is to determine the average cap rates for the area based on comparable properties that have sold recently. Another way to determine a cap rate is to select one based on your minimum return requirement. If 8 percent is the lowest cap rate you'd accept, dividing a property's current NOI by 0.08 will enable you to arrive at the price you'd be willing to pay for the property.

$$\frac{\text{Net operating income}}{\text{Cap rate}} = \text{Price} \quad \text{or} \quad \frac{\$27,000}{0.08} = \$337,500$$

Don't let anyone convince you that the property is worth anything more than the current NOI divided by an acceptable cap rate. Don't overpay for the property's potential; pay only for its current performance.

During the years when many apartment buildings were being converted into condominiums, many traditional apartment investors faced a severely compressed cap rate environment, with 4 or 5 percent caps being the norm in most condo-crazed coastal towns. During the next few years, as we work through the downturn in the market, I expect a 300-basis-point (3 percent) increase in caps (i.e., prices will decline, as there is an inverse relationship between cap rates and prices) in some areas of the country.

The value of the property (or the purchase price) does not take debt service (paying the mortgage) into account. In fact, the cap provides a yield on capital, assuming that the property has no debt. This allows investors to compare properties across the board regardless of the terms of their financing. Although mortgage debt must be considered when calculating your cash flow and overall return, it is not a factor that influences the cap rate.

Defined: A *basis point* is equal to 1/100th of 1 percent—1 percent equals 100 basis points, and 0.01 percent = 1 basis point.

High Vacancy Rates

If you are acquiring a value-add deal, the vacancy rate at the time of your analysis might be higher than the average for similar properties in the same area. A very good strategy to reduce your risk with an underperforming property is to negotiate a provision that the date of closing will take place once the property's occupancy rate reaches an acceptable figure. I once purchased a large apartment complex in which the occupancy rate upon signing the sales contract was 70 percent. The stabilized occupancy rate was closer to 90 percent. I inserted a clause in the sales contract that required the closing to take place 30 days after the owners achieved 90 percent occupancy. The contract also gave me the authority to review the applications and credit reports of prospective tenants and reject applicants who did not meet specific standards. This simple strategy enables you to reduce the uncertainties associated with high-vacancy-rate properties.

Cash Flow Analysis

After calculating a property's value based on the income approach, you'll need to estimate the future cash flows that the property will produce, to determine the property's overall return during the holding period.

Net operating income (NOI)
Less: Debt service
Equals: Cash flow before tax (CFBT)

Case Studies: 3-, 40-, and 205-Unit Apartment Complexes

In the following pages, I will explain how to analyze three properties.

Case Study 1: Three Units

I received the following e-mail from an investor who was soliciting my advice regarding a three-unit apartment building he was considering.

Hi Matt,

I bought and read your book, *2 Years to a Million in Real Estate*—an excellent book with practical advice. I'm using your analysis to conduct my due diligence on a small apartment building. Unfortunately, the cash flow will be negative from the very first day and will likely remain that way for the first year. The debt service looks like the killer, but it appears to be about the best I can find. Based on these numbers, I'm considering pulling the plug on the purchase.

This is the information on a property I am looking at purchasing. What do you think?

Kevin
Columbus, OH

Investing in Apartment Buildings

VALUATION WORKSHEET

Property overview:
Property size: Three-unit apartment building
Occupancy: 100 percent rented
Location: Columbus, Ohio
Proposed purchase price: $162,500

	Per Month	Per Year
Rent	$1,700.00	$20,400.00
Less vacancy (5%)	$85.00	$1,020.00
Net rental income	$1,615.00	$19,380.00
Plus other income	$50.00	$600.00
Effective gross income	$1,665.00	$19,980.00
Operating Expenses		
Taxes	$314.00	$3,678.00
Insurance	$95.77	$1,149.24
Water and sewer	$40.00	$480.00
Repairs and maintenance	$50.00	$600.00
Miscellaneous expenses	$50.00	$600.00
Property management	$119.00	$1,428.00
Total annual operating expenses*	$668.77	$8,025.24
Net operating income	$996.23	$11,954.76
Cap rate		7.3567%
Debt service*	$1,057.27	$12,687.24
Cash flow	-$61.04	-$732.48

Note: The investor did not include expenses for trash removal, landscaping/snow removal, or advertising. The investor calculated his own monthly debt service obligation based on the rates and terms provided by his local bank.

If you had read my first book, you'd already know my response to this investor's inquiry. If the property doesn't generate a positive cash flow with a reasonable down payment, you should avoid buying it unless there's a fairly quick and painless way of making it cash flow positive (this assumes that you're a noninstitutional investor, because these deep-pocketed firms are better equipped to hold and improve properties with negative cash flow if the overall return during the holding period is satisfactory).

This investor later asked whether he should put more money down to create a positive cash flow by reducing his debt obligation. My suggestion was that if a property with a 20 percent down payment fails to generate a positive cash flow (i.e., a negative return), I would recommend that he steer clear of the property if there's no significant upside or value-add play in sight. That said, even if this investor acquires the property in cash (i.e., with no mortgage), creating a positive annual cash flow of $11,954.76, this property will unlikely warrant the use of his capital. This leads to the next question, which is whether the property can generate a superior return given alternative investment choices.

> *Defined: Leverage* is the use of loans to finance real estate investments. A real estate investment that does not involve the use of borrowed funds for acquisition purposes is referred to as *unleveraged*.

Case Study 2: 40-Unit Deal

The following is the analysis of a 40-unit apartment complex:

Overview

Price	$3,000,000
# of units	40
Price/unit	$75,000
Rentable SF	22,350
Price per SF	$134
Cap rate	6.90%
Year built	1965
Lot size	29,900

Scheduled Income

# of Units	Unit Type	SF	Total SF	Current Rents	Monthly Income
10	STUDIO	310	3000	$745	$7,450
6	1/1	625	3250	$816	$4,900 *
24	1/1 LOFTS	650	15000	$890	$21,350 *
40			22550		$33,700

*Numbers were rounded

Percentage	Source of Capital	Amount	Parts	Annual Payments
50%	Owner financing	$1,500,000	6%	$90,000
50%	Cash down	$1,500,000		

Annualized Operating Income	
Income	**Current**
Gross scheduled income	$404,400
Less: V&C loss	20,220
Net rental income	$384,180
Plus: other income	$3,200
Effective gross income	**$387,380**
Expenses	
Real estate taxes	$71,274
Insurance	$36,000
Utilities	$23,866
Pool	$2,000
Waste removal	$7,100
Pest control	$1,500
Management	$19,369
Repairs & maintenance	$19,369
Total operating expenses	**$180,478**
as a % of EGI	47%
NOI	**$206,902**
Debt service	$90,000
Cash flow	$116,902

Additional Ratios

Cash-on-Cash Return: This ratio shows how the remaining cash after all operating expenses and mortgages are paid compares to the initial amount of capital invested to acquire the property:

$$\text{Cash-on-cash return} = \frac{\text{Annual cash flow}}{\text{Initial cash investment}}$$

$$\text{Cash-on-cash return} = \frac{\$116,900}{\$1,500,000}$$

$$\text{Cash-on-cash return} = 7.79\%$$

Debt Service Coverage Ratio (DSCR): This ratio shows how the net operating income compares to the debt service. Banks and other lending institutions typically prefer a DSCR of 1.2 or greater—the property's NOI must be at least 20 percent more than the annual mortgage payments—for the bank to underwrite the deal and approve financing.

Because of the leverage being used on this particular project, the DSCR was far greater than the 1.2 threshold.

$$\text{Debt service coverage ratio} = \frac{\text{NOI}}{\text{debt service}}$$

$$\text{Debt service coverage ratio} = \frac{\$206{,}902}{\$90{,}000}$$

$$\text{Debt service coverage ratio} = 2.3$$

The higher the ratio, the easier it is for the borrower to pay the mortgage on an income-producing property.

Case Study 3: 205-Unit Apartment Complex (Institutional Deal)

Now let's take a look at a much larger property. This apartment complex consisted of 205 units, and the owners were extremely motivated to sell because it was a failed condo conversion project. A small group of investors acquired this property at the height of the condo conversion craze. The owners were rather sanguine about the prospect of generating handsome returns after preselling (writing contracts and accepting deposits for) 112 units within the first 12 months of ownership. Unfortunately, the renovations took longer than anticipated, and many of the tenants were uncooperative in moving out of their rental units. By the time the developers had completed the work and received their certificate of occupancy (CO), the buyers who held contracts on units either were reluctant to close, given the less favorable market conditions, or couldn't obtain financing because of the tighter lending restrictions after the credit crunch. At the end of the day, none of the initial buyers closed on their units.

After paying a premium for the property and investing millions of dollars in unit renovations and capital improvements, the owners were left with a nearly vacant property, producing a very small revenue stream, with few prospective condo buyers in sight. Meanwhile, operating expenses such as taxes, insurance, water, electricity, garbage removal, landscaping, maintenance, and so on still had to be paid, along with a significant mortgage payment each month. Because the owners could not sell individual units (the condo market no longer existed because of the subprime crisis, which resulted in much stricter lending standards) and the rental income (even at 100 percent occupancy) could not support the property's existing debt structure and ongoing operating expenses, there were no viable exit strategies. The owners were losing close to $200,000 each month, or nearly $7,000 a day, so they stopped making mortgage payments and defaulted on their loan. After 90 days of nonpayments, the lender's special assets division took action.

As previously discussed, representatives from the special assets division typically pursue one or more of the following options:

1. Attempt to negotiate a payment plan with the owners.
2. Pursue foreclosure procedures.
3. Attempt to find a buyer for the property (short sale).

The bank determined that the current appraised value of the property was less than the outstanding balance on the loan. Also, realistically, prospective buyers would not consider the sale of condos as a viable exit strategy when underwriting this deal. Instead, buyers of this asset would need to determine the property's worth based on its fundamentals as a rental property. Also, lending institutions would underwrite and approve the loan only if the property made financial sense as a rental property; it would be challenging to secure financing otherwise.

Understanding What's to Come

In instances such as this, a prospective buyer must negotiate directly with the senior lender. Your hope is that the bank will accept a reasonable price so that you can buy the property, operate it as a rental community, and make enough to achieve your minimum return. In this case, the bank wanted the owners to sign a deficiency note for the difference between our offer and the balance of the outstanding loan. Since the owners were not in a position to write any more checks, the lender would have to either accept our offer and take an immediate loss (to the tune of several million dollars) or foreclose on the property and likely take a loss in the future. Once the regulators take control (and I suspect they will by the first or second quarter of 2009), the FDIC will force lenders to liquidate the nonperforming loans on their balance sheets and mark to market the prices on all assets, and groups like mine (opportunity and "vulture" funds) will pile in with billions of dollars to buy apartment complexes.

The following graph shows the delinquency rates on loans held by commercial banks in 2007. The numbers are alarming and will certainly increase during the next few years.

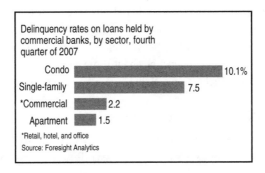

Elizabeth MacDonald wrote in one of her financial blogs, "After the S&L crisis, market regulators and accountants cracked down on inflated real estate valuations rampant during that binge period and demanded new accounting rules forcing instant price-tagging of all assets based on what the market would immediately deliver." The chairman of the House Financial Services Committee, Barney Frank (D-Mass), is working with regulators to determine what should be done. Everyone, including Frank, is worried about the financial chaos and the train wreck that many industry insiders feel is imminent.

Internal Rate of Return

Before meeting with the lender, I had to analyze the numbers carefully to determine what the property was worth on a rental basis before making an offer. At the time, I was working in conjunction with a private

Investing in Apartment Buildings

equity firm to evaluate the property and make an offer to the bank. Institutional investors tend to make acquisitions based on internal rate of return (IRR) calculations, or the overall return based on a series of projected cash flows.

> *Note:* IRR can be used to rank the projects you are analyzing. Assuming that all other factors are the same, the project with the highest projected IRR would probably offer the best overall return.

Warren Buffett evaluates companies in the same way. As quoted by Robert Hagstrom in *The Warren Buffett Way*, Mr. Buffett said,

> To properly value a business, you should ideally take all of the flows of money that will be distributed between now and judgment day and discount them at an appropriate discount rate. That's what valuing businesses is all about. Part of the equation is how confident you can be about those cash flows occurring. We try to look at businesses that are predictable.

Mr. Buffett's methodology for analyzing companies is no different from the way you should determine the value of apartment buildings. Understanding the property's expected cash flows during the holding period and determining its return on your equity is how institutions value prospective acquisition targets.

Overview

Total number of units	205
Units sold	0
Units available	205
Vacancies	67
Rented	138
Current vacancy rate	33%
Price per unit	$105,000
Purchase price	$21,525,000
LTV	50%
Debt (50% of purchase price)	$10,762,500
Interest rate (interest only)	7.00%
Annual debt service	$753,375

Due Diligence

	Current year	%	Year 1	Year 2	Year 3	Year 4	Year 5
Operating Revenues							
Gross scheduled income	$1,874,415		$2,784,457	$2,867,991	$2,954,031	$3,042,652	$3,133,931
Less vacancy & collections			$(891,026)	$(229,439)	$(206,782)	$(212,986)	$(219,375)
Net rental income	$1,874,415		$1,893,431	$2,638,552	$2,747,249	$2,829,666	$2,914,556
Other income (laundry)	$16,200		$16,686	$17,187	$17,702	$18,233	$18,780
Effective gross income	$1,890,615		$1,910,117	$2,655,738	$2,764,951	$2,847,899	$2,933,336
Operating Expenses							
Property management	$75,625	4.00%	111,378	114,720	118,161	121,706	125,357
Payroll	$30,000	1.59%	125,000	128,750	132,613	136,591	140,689
Marketing/advertising	$25,000	1.32%	60,000	61,800	63,654	65,564	67,531
Credit reports	$1,495	0.08%	1,540	1,586	1,634	1,683	1,733
Extermination service	$6,480	0.34%	6,674	6,875	7,081	7,293	7,512
Working compensation	$12,844	0.68%	13,229	13,626	14,035	14,456	14,890
Property insurance	$239,015	12.64%	184,500	190,035	195,736	201,608	207,656
Licenses and permits	$2,789	0.15%	2,873	2,959	3,048	3,139	3,233
Postage	$345	0.02%	355	366	377	388	400
Accounting and tax services	$12,143	0.64%	12,507	12,883	13,269	13,667	14,077
Pool maintenance	$6,720	0.36%	6,922	7,129	7,343	7,563	7,790
Lawn and landscaping	$19,200	1.02%	19,776	20,369	20,980	21,610	22,258
Building materials	$3,272	0.17%	3,370	3,471	3,575	3,683	3,793
Plumbing repairs	$1,460	0.08%	1,504	1,549	1,595	1,643	1,693
Telephone	$3,586	0.19%	3,694	3,804	3,919	4,036	4,157
Gas	$37,562	1.99%	38,689	39,850	41,045	42,276	43,545
Electricity	$21,236	1.12%	21,873	22,529	23,205	23,901	24,618
Water and sewer	$95,320	5.04%	104,852	107,998	111,237	114,575	118,012
Garbage disposal	$23,754	1.26%	24,467	25,935	27,491	28,315	29,165
Fire alarm	$6,676	0.35%	6,876	7,083	7,295	7,514	7,739
Property taxes	$357,779	18.92%	430,500	443,415	456,717	470,419	484,532
Total operating expenses	$982,301		$1,180,579	$1,216,731	$1,254,010	$1,291,631	$1,330,380
Operating exp as a % of EGI		52%	62%	46%	45%	45%	45%
Net Operating Income	$908,315		$729,538	$1,439,008	$1,510,940	$1,556,268	$1,602,957

		Year 1	Year 2	Year 3	Year 4	Year 5
Annual debt service		$753,375	$753,375	$753,375	$753,375	$753,375
Cash flow		$(23,837)	$685,633	$757,565	$802,893	$849,582

IRR Analysis		Year 1	Year 2	Year 3	Year 4	Year 5
IRR	15.17%					
Invested capital		$(10,762,500)				
Rental proceeds		$(23,837)	$685,633	$757,565	$802,893	$849,582
Sales proceeds						$15,151,964
Totals		$(10,786,337)	$685,633	$757,565	$802,893	$16,001,546

Sale End of Year 5	
NOI	$1,602,957
Cap rate	6.00%
Sales price	$26,715,942
Sales commissions	$801,478
0.03	
Net sales	$25,914,464
Debt	$10,762,500
Net $	$15,151,964

As you will see from this case study, the IRR provides a worthy measure of value for real estate investments.

The information about the property is as follows:

Investing in Apartment Buildings

At first glance, these spreadsheets may seem rather daunting if you've never been exposed to these calculations, but upon further inspection, you'll find that the analysis is rather simple.

Understanding the Analysis

The "current year" numbers were provided by the seller.

The average monthly rent per unit was approximately $1,131. The average rent multiplied by the total number of units multiplied by 12 months in the year gives the gross scheduled income in Year 1.

> Gross scheduled income in Year 1 = average monthly rent × number of units × 12 months.

Or,

$$\$1,131 \times 205 \times 12 = \$2,784,457$$

(The average rent and the GSI were rounded. Otherwise, the GSI would equal $2,782,260.)

Vacancy and collection loss were 32 percent in Year 1, 8 percent in Year 2, and 7 percent a year thereafter. These, of course, were our assumptions.

Rental revenue increased by 3 percent during Years 2 through 5.

Operating expenses (with the exception of waste disposal) increased by 3 percent during Years 2 through 5. Property management fees were 4 percent of gross scheduled income. I prefer that the property management fee be based on EGI because it takes into account vacancy and collection losses as well as any ancillary income.

Annual debt service was calculated by taking the loan amount of $10,762,500 (or 50 percent of the purchase price in this case) and multiplying it by an interest-only rate of 7 percent.

So,

$$\$10,762,500 \times 0.07 = \$753,375$$

The sale of the property takes place at the end of Year 5 at a 6 percent cap rate.

Due Diligence

The sale price is calculated as follows:

$$\frac{\text{Net operating income (in Year 5)}}{\text{Cap rate of 6\%}}$$

or

$$\$1,602,957/0.06 = \$26,715.942$$

Numbers were rounded; otherwise the actual NOI would be $1,602,956.54.

Broker's commissions in the amount of 3 percent are deducted from the sales price.

We would secure an interest-only loan in the amount of $10,762,500 (for 50 percent of the purchase price). Therefore, in Year 5, the total balance would be due upon the sale.

The determination of value for our group was based primarily on the IRR for the property during a five-year holding period. As you can see from the previous analysis, the property generated five different cash flows. In Year 1, a negative cash flow of $10,786,337 includes the down payment of $10,762,500 and a $23,837 negative cash flow from the property. Years 2 through 4 show positive annual cash flows from the property. And the fifth and final year assumes a positive cash flow of $849,582 from the property and the net sales proceeds from the sale of the property in the amount of $15,151,964.

As previously discussed, annual cash flows are calculated as follows:

Effective gross income
Less: Operating expenses
Equals: Net operating income
Less: Debt service
Equals: Annual cash flow

Using Microsoft Excel, you easily can calculate the IRR for a given project if you know the annual cash flows. The threshold for us was an

IRR of 15 percent, so at $105,000 a unit we'd achieve our desired return.

Congratulations! You survived the longest chapter in the book and learned a lot in the process. Due diligence is perhaps the most important component of your future success as a real estate investor, so this was time well spent.

Chapter Summary

- Due diligence is a means for verifying all of the assumptions and facts about a property before making the purchase.
- Due diligence consists of a third-party inspection (environmental site assessment and property condition assessment) as well as your own qualitative and quantitative review.
- Be sure to speak with everyone who is familiar with the property. Each person who lives or works at the property should be considered a credible source of valuable information.
- Verify each piece of data given to you, and assume that none of the information provided by the owner or broker is accurate.
- Use current numbers and your own projections to determine the value of a property.

8

Financing and Acquisition

Creditors have better memories than debtors.
—Proverb

What You're About to Learn

- The reality of today's tighter lending standards
- How to secure financing for multifamily acquisitions
- Understanding debt service coverage ratios
- The importance of loan-to-value ratios
- How lenders underwrite loans

There are five major components of real estate investing:

1. Finding deals
2. Evaluating (or underwriting) deals
3. Financing deals
4. Managing properties
5. Selling properties

This chapter will focus on the third component, financing deals. You've already determined the size of the property that works best for you, selected a farm area, found a value-add project, and performed your due diligence. Now you need to secure financing, close on the property, and take ownership.

Before a bank approves any loan, it must review the loan application and apply several financial models that measure risk. Banks have well-staffed departments dedicated to *underwriting* each loan. The decision to provide debt financing must be weighed carefully, balancing the risk that a bank assumes when it lends capital (for the acquisition of a real estate asset) against the benefits associated with the profit made from providing the loan.

> *Defined:* Bank underwriting is the process of determining a bank's credit risk in funding a loan.

Financing Before and Financing Now

At the height of the last real estate frenzy (2001–2007), obtaining financing for nearly any project was facilitated by less stringent underwriting standards and more liberal lending practices. Cheap and easy debt was readily available. The financial ratios that lenders had historically used to examine the risk profile of a loan applicant no longer applied, and thus financial institutions approved many applicants who could not afford to pay their mortgages. Credit problems ensued when subprime borrowers began defaulting on their loans, and the subsequent credit tightening in the residential arena began to seep into the commercial marketplace. Bear Stearns was the first major investment banking institution to fall victim to the credit crisis, on March 16, 2008, but it won't be the last.

Figure 8.1 shows how the value of Bear Stearns dropped precipitously during the first two weeks of March.

In the aftermath, there are significant challenges for anyone who currently needs to finance condos, single-family homes, multifamily properties, and even commercial properties. No one is certain how long these problems will persist, but the new reality may be with us for several more years. Today, lending guidelines are much more rigid, as the credit markets have frozen and the real estate debt market has dried up. Banks are no longer willing to approve loans unless there's significant equity in the property (i.e., you must put more money down).

During the boom, banks were accustomed to lending 90 to 100 percent of the purchase price for a small residential multifamily property, and they typically would lend 80 percent of the price for a large multifamily property. Nowadays, those percentages have decreased to 80 per-

Figure 8.1   Bear Stearns' stock value

cent or less for small residential multifamily properties and 70 percent or less for most large multifamily loans. Lenders today must be confident that there's plenty of surplus equity because, if the market continues to decline, they don't want to own a property that is worth less than the outstanding loan balance. Instead, they'll want to sell the property for at least the par value of the outstanding note, so they must take the necessary precautions to reduce their risk exposure.

I recently had a meeting with the vice president of commercial lending at one of the largest banks in Florida. His group approves all commercial lending for multifamily acquisitions at that bank. I was not surprised to learn that his group had approved only two loans during the past three quarters.

He explained: "The DSCR (debt service coverage ratio) on most of the applications we've received has not met our 1.25 criterion unless investors have a 40 to 50 percent LTV (loan-to-value ratio). Because of our new lending standards, the numbers simply don't make sense on a rental basis unless the buyers are putting significantly more money into their deals."

Because banks now are burdened by tremendous losses from nonperforming residential and commercial loans, they are reluctant to approve new loans, making the financing of properties increasingly difficult. Increased equity requirements mean that investors will need to reach deeper into their own pockets to finance transactions. Tighter loan underwriting standards and development projects that have to be canceled because of the lack of available financing will be the norm, not the exception, during the next few years. However, large institutions and savvy entrepreneurs who have cash on hand and have been sitting on the sidelines waiting for this crisis to occur will find themselves in an enviable position.

Motivated sellers will be more prevalent in the marketplace in the years to come. Because most investors will require financing but won't be able to get it during these more credit-restrictive times, there will be less competition on the buy side. Cash will be king (as it always is) during this down-market cycle.

Financing Properties

Because real estate assets with fewer than five units are considered by lenders to be residential properties and can be financed as such, it should remain easier to obtain loans for these projects using traditional mortgage lenders with conventional mortgage programs. Also, the availability of higher loan-to-value ratios for properties with four units or less should remain far greater than for their larger multifamily counterparts.

As noted earlier, the requirements for commercial loans are usually more stringent, and the rates tend to be higher. The financial institutions making loans on larger properties rely on rental income to service the debt. If the units are not rented, the property is mismanaged for any length of time, or the applicant is an inexperienced buyer, a problem may arise that will make it difficult for the borrower to repay the loan. Lenders are aware of the inherent challenges and increased risks associated with larger apartment buildings, so they've made it more difficult to gain approval for these loans.

Multifamily Financing

Lenders determine the value of multifamily properties and subsequently establish loan amounts for those assets using several variables that may not be readily apparent to a borrower. The remaining pages in this chapter provide a conceptual understanding of the ways in which lenders approach the underwriting of multifamily loans.

All lending institutions are different, and their guidelines are continually changing; however, there are some general guidelines and terms that you should be familiar with before you finance a property.

Maximum LTV

- Typical lending programs offer financing at 70 to 80 percent of value (or 70 to 80 percent LTV).
- Secondary financing (or junior debt) providing a combined LTV of 80 to 90 percent might be allowed but is less likely during this credit crunch.

• Some programs allow the seller to carry back a second mortgage (5 to 10 percent of the purchase price in seller financing) that will be subordinate to the first mortgage.

Debt Service Coverage Ratio

The debt service coverage ratio is a widely used financial benchmark that measures an income-producing property's ability to cover its annual debt (mortgage payments). The DSCR is calculated by dividing the net operating income by a property's annual debt service, or the annual total of all interest and principal payments paid on all loans on a property (although many senior lenders will consider only their own first loan). A DSCR of less than 1.2 (for example) indicates that the income generated by a property might be insufficient to cover the mortgage payments.

A DSCR of 0.90 indicates a negative cash flow. In this instance, the income available after paying all operating expenses is only enough to cover 90 percent of the annual mortgage payments. A property with a DSCR of 1.20 generates 20 percent more income than is required by the annual debt service. Lenders are typically comfortable with having 20 to 25 percent more income available.

As an example, let's assume that you are contemplating the purchase of an investment property with a net operating income of $120,000 and annual debt service of $100,000. The DSCR for this property would be 1.2. This means that the property would generate 20 percent more annual net operating income (or $20,000) than is required to cover the annual mortgage payments.

$$DSCR = \frac{\text{net operating income}}{\text{annual debt service}} = \frac{\$120,000}{\$100,000} = 1.2$$

All lending institutions require that an income-producing property meet their minimum debt service coverage ratios for a loan to be approved. DSCR requirements for lending institutions can vary from as low as 1.1 to as high as 1.5. From a lending institution's point of view, the higher the DSCR, the more income there is to cover the debt service and, thus, the less risk involved in the deal.

Appraised Value

Even when a property comfortably passes the prescribed DSCR hurdle, there are other parameters that lenders employ that may restrict the loan amount. The acceptable capitalization rate is one factor, and another is the lender's third-party appraisal (determination of property value) using the income approach. An institution could give greater importance to one or the other, thereby affecting the approval of the loan.

Term

The most common loan programs offer terms of 3, 5, 7, 10, 15, 20, 25, and 30 years. Interest-only (although less common in down markets) and balloon notes are also available.

Rates

Rates depend on the lending institution, the nature of the loan, and the asset being financed. Shop around for the best terms and rates, because not all lenders offer the same programs, and rates can vary quite dramatically from one lender to the next.

Prepayment Penalties

With commercial loans, the penalty for paying off a loan early (prepayment penalty) typically decreases each year. For example, if the entire balance of the loan is paid off in the first year, a penalty of 5 percent of the outstanding balance could be owed. Prepayment in the second year could incur a 4 percent penalty, prepayment in the third year a 3 percent penalty, and so on (5 percent, 4 percent, 3 percent, 2 percent, and 1 percent).

Recourse

Commercial loan programs may require recourse (a personal guaranty). It's advantageous from an investor's perspective to obtain a nonrecourse loan because with such a loan, you have only your equity in the property at risk; none of your personal assets are at risk should you default on the loan. If the borrower defaults on a nonrecourse loan, the lender can seize the collateral (the property), but its recovery is limited only to the property that the loan was made on.

Closing Costs

Borrowers are responsible for all due diligence and closing costs. Some of the costs associated with a loan may include a property appraisal, ESA (Phase I environmental), title report, and other such costs. It's not uncommon for the closing costs to run to tens of thousands of dollars for large multifamily properties.

The financial marketplace is continuously changing. To find the best loan for your specific needs, you'll need to conduct a thorough investigation of all your options. There are numerous lenders and brokers who will be willing to finance your multifamily projects, but it will take a serious effort on your behalf to find the best program for your particular needs.

At the back of this book, you'll find a complete list of the top multifamily lenders in the country. Contact them directly to learn more about their specific lending programs.

Chapter Summary

- With the onset of the subprime problems and tighter lending practices, obtaining financing for income-producing properties has become increasingly more difficult.
- Lenders are requiring investors to have more equity in their deals, so they are now providing loans at significantly lower LTVs.
- Most lenders require a minimum DSCR of 1.2 or greater.
- Lenders determine the value of apartment buildings through a property appraisal that uses the income approach.
- Not all lenders are created equal. Shop around for the best loans, terms, and rates that meet your specific needs.

9

Property Management

Look at a day when you are supremely satisfied
at the end. It's not a day when you lounge
around doing nothing; it's when you've had
everything to do, and you've done it.
— MARGARET THATCHER

What You're About to Learn

- How landlords differ from investors
- Assuming the property manager's responsibilities
- Hiring a property manager
- Local versus national property management companies
- Hiring your own staff
- Managing from afar
- Managing the manager
- Compensating a property manager or management company
- Reporting
- Achieving results

If you've made it this far in the book, I know you're committed to investing in apartment buildings. At this point, you've successfully located, analyzed, negotiated, and closed on a property. Now, it's time to roll up your sleeves and get your hands dirty.

During the due diligence period, you undoubtedly became familiar with your apartment building, but now that the previous owner is no longer in the picture, you're about to become even more familiar with it. Calls will start coming in from tenants, and issues that you have not anticipated may arise. After taking a complete inventory of your new asset, immediately start to implement your value-add strategy, and don't stop until you've reached your objectives.

To increase the property's NOI, a sound plan must be executed with great precision. Achieving high returns is of paramount importance, so everything that you and your property manager do should be directed toward obtaining results. Because the property manager is the captain of this particular ship (keeping with this metaphor, you would be the commander in chief), he decides where to steer the ship, how best to manage the crew, and how to arrive safely at the next destination. Property managers are in a position to make or break your business, so pay close attention to this chapter because you must quickly learn how to keep them motivated, enthusiastic, and aligned with your objectives. Significant equity can be manufactured from the very first moment you take possession of a property right up to the day you sell it. The manager's job is to maximize that equity, so you must choose your captain wisely and keep him motivated and on course.

Should I Manage My Own Properties?

If you're buying a residential multifamily property and are relatively new to the business, I recommend that you assume the manager's role. On the other hand, if you are already an experienced, seasoned, or institutional investor, you will probably hire your own on-site managers or sign a contract with a third-party management company to handle the day-to-day activities.

In my opinion, all new investors should perform their own property management duties (assuming that the investor can manage the requirements of his day job in addition to the new responsibilities of being a landlord). You'll quickly learn the challenges that confront full-time managers as they stabilize a property and carry out a value-add strategy. Roof repairs, broken windows, and malfunctioning heating and cooling systems are normal occurrences in apartment buildings. When you've dealt with all these issues personally, you'll better understand how to budget for and/or avoid these problems with future acquisitions. Furthermore, this knowledge will be extremely useful when you are hiring a manager or a vendor. Managing a property will give you the opportunity to gain invaluable experience. Only after you've fielded all the tenant phone calls, screened each new prospective tenant, filled all vacancies, organized repairs with vendors, paid all the outstanding invoices, and stabilized the property will you understand fully the wide range of challenges that comes hand in hand with owning income-producing properties. More important, you'll better understand how much repairs actually cost, how long each type of repair or maintenance job takes on average to complete, how best to deal with disgruntled tenants, and how to maximize fully the economic potential of a given property. If you lack this firsthand knowledge, an unscrupulous property manager could easily take advantage of you. It's a good idea to "walk in the shoes" of a property manager for a few months or even years, especially since you will eventually be overseeing property managers in the future.

Landlords versus Investors

What's the difference between a landlord and a real estate investor?

I define a *landlord* as an individual who manages his own properties day to day. He fields all phone calls from tenants; he coordinates repairs with vendors, screens prospective tenants, fills vacancies, inspects units, and does all the other necessary tasks. In other words, he deals with all of the headaches associated with rental property management. In contrast, my definition of a real estate *investor* is someone who hires a competent property manager to oversee his properties so that he can work on the next deal. The investor is not burdened by daily interactions with tenants and property issues. Instead, he is engaged in obtaining financing and acquiring and closing on the next great opportunity rather than being distracted from managing the day-to-day operations of each investment property.

The natural progression from landlord to investor might take a few years, so don't rush this important process. Gain experience at the ground level (some might say cut your teeth) by doing it yourself and then, after you're ready for greater challenges, hire someone as your property manager. A real estate investor ultimately delegates the daily management responsibility to others so that he can devote his limited time and energy to building a larger and more profitable real estate portfolio.

Hiring a Property Management Company or Property Manager

The experience you gain by managing your own properties will enable you to be a better judge of character later on—a skill that you will need when you make the decision to hire professional management.

There are quite a few property management companies to choose from in every market; however, it's best to have a Certified Property Manager (CPM) at the helm. CPM is a designation awarded by the Institute of Real Estate Management (IREM) to the top professionals in this industry.

Web site: A list of CPMs nationwide can be found at www.irem.org.

There are three options available for hiring companies to manage income-producing properties:

1. *Hire a national property management firm.* These firms usually have a minimum unit criterion as well as a minimum monthly

payment. They offer tremendous support staff, back-office accounting capabilities, extensive experience, and proprietary systems. These companies may already be managing thousands of units nationwide (including some of their own assets, which very well might compete with your inventory).

2. *Hire a local property management company.* These companies are based in the city or state where your property is located and, in my experience, tend to be slightly more affordable than the national firms. They will have intimate knowledge of the local market. Unfortunately, they also tend to have less support staff, fewer resources, and, often, their own portfolio of local apartments. Both national and local management companies will assign a property manager to oversee your asset and could hire an on-site manager to deal with the daily operations (depending on the number of units you own). The on-site manager reports directly to the property manager.

3. *Assemble your own property management team.* You can hire your own property manager. This person might be the manager of a nearby property (at least, that's how I have found such people in the past). They typically prefer to bring their own on-site maintenance crew and leasing assistants with them. In this case, the on-site property manager reports directly to you and is accountable only to you.

> *Web site:* Search here for management companies:
> http://www.allpropertymanagement.com.

For the record, I prefer option 3 because I have greater control when I select a staff that is directly accountable to me, and I eliminate any additional and unnecessary layers of reporting. Also, I avoid any conflicts of interest: most management companies have their own portfolios of rentals, and I don't ever want to worry about the possibility that their properties will have priority over mine.

> *Note:* The following is an e-mail from an astute investor regarding the hiring of a national or local property management group versus establishing your own.
>
> Matt:
>
> I do not want to use a national property management group . . . one of the reasons for our success with real estate is our control of every part of the process . . . we know to the penny what is happening . . . we control the manner in which tenants are treated and the quality of the services, etc.

Although there are many superb, professional, and competent mangers, be sure to check all their personal and professional references, work experience, and background. That way, you'll be sure to make the best possible decision. After all, your property manager represents you, and should he use poor judgment by doing something illegal or inappropriate, you could be responsible for his actions.

Hiring a Property Management Firm or Establishing Your Own Team

When it is time to select a property management company or create one of your own, there are some important questions to ask before you make your final decision.

- How many years of experience does the manager or property management company have?
- Who will be responsible for the day-to-day activities?
- Does the management company have its own maintenance crew, or does it work with subcontractors? What are the hourly rates for their work?
- How many buildings does the company own and manage in the area?
- Does it own similar units (e.g., similar two-bedroom units in the same part of town)?

Property Management

- Will its properties compete with yours?
- What is the priority given to vacancies at properties it may own? If someone calls its office inquiring about a two-bedroom unit, how can you be assured that your property will receive as much attention as the company's own units?

> *Note:* The vast majority of the time, the units that a property management company owns will have priority over your vacant apartments, so set your expectations accordingly. This might not be fair, but it's the reality of doing business with a firm that both owns properties and provides third-party management services in your farm area.

- What are the company's qualifications? Does it have a CPM certification?
- What's the manager or company's strategy for filling vacancies and stabilizing your property? The manager's ability to rent units is extremely important. You always can hire out maintenance, but renting units and keeping them rented is critical to your success.
- What's the manager's or company's plan of action for emergencies and/or any other tenant-related issues?
- How quickly can the manager or company respond to tenant problems?
- What's the manager's or firm's plan to reduce costs, increase rents, and improve your property's NOI?
- Does it have relationships with vendors who can provide services at reduced rates?
- What is the company's current portfolio vacancy or (in the case of a single property manager) the vacancy of the property he manages?
- How many units does the company manage?
- What does the firm charge for its services?
- Does it have 24-hour service for tenants?
- What legal counsel does the firm use, and do these lawyers specialize in landlord-tenant law?

- Does the company offer real-time and online reporting?
- Is its estimated budget for the property reasonable and in line with your expectations and timeline?
- Can the manager or firm provide a sample monthly report for your perusal?

It makes sense to ask the management firm for an annual budget. The firm probably will invest the time needed to prepare this only after you have committed to it, but establishing one within the first month of ownership should be a priority. Afterward, you'll need to obtain monthly financial and operational reports from the firm. Be sure to establish goals that are achievable. If they are not reached, call other local property managers to determine whether this is a management issue or a systemic challenge throughout the entire market. You may need to adjust your goals periodically if you are in an economically unstable location or if the market is fundamentally changing.

Compensating a Property Manager

National, local, and privately hired professional property managers charge between 3 and 10 percent of the gross rents (depending on the size of your property), plus commissions for filling vacancies and bonuses for outstanding performance and supervising major renovations.

I prefer to pay at the lower end of that scale while offering an incentive package that enables the manager to earn much more. This is accomplished by offering incentives in the form of bonuses and commissions if a manager achieves my objectives. Just make sure that the objectives are well defined, achievable, and measurable.

Note: A friend of mine offers his manager an incentive that includes a 35 percent revenue share on the entire positive cash flow (the funds remaining after paying the mortgage). That way, he knows that the mortgage will be paid every month, and he and his property manager are always aligned with regard to the financial performance of the property.

Property Management

A complete compensation package for a manger could be made up of the following: salary or a percentage of the property's income or profit, benefits, cell phone, an apartment at no cost, bonuses, and commissions.

This is an example of a typical compensation package at one of my properties:

- Income: 4 percent of EGI
- Commissions: $100 for each unit rented (assistants earn $50 per unit)
- Monthly bonus: $500 bonus for maintaining a 95 percent occupancy rate
- Benefits: health insurance
- Apartment: free of charge
- Cell phone: free of charge

Managing from Afar

If you are not local (which I don't recommend unless you are a seasoned investor), you'll need to visit the property as frequently as possible. Frequent visits are required if the property is not stabilized. Periodic phone conversations with the manager help to address any ongoing issues.

If you are having trouble obtaining real answers from the property manager or doubt his honesty, consider hiring a "secret shopper" to tour your property. Such a scout can give you a report on the performance of your on-site manager. A secret or mystery shopper poses as a prospective tenant and contacts your manager, inquiring about available units. He then tours the property, enters units, asks a host of questions, and reports back to you regarding his overall experience. Secret shoppers can be used to evaluate

- Customer service
- Management's professionalism or lack thereof
- The leasing agent's knowledge of the property and follow-up
- The cleanliness of units, disrepair, neglect, and other such issues

According to the Mystery Shopping Providers Association, mystery shopping is the practice of using shoppers who have been specially briefed to anonymously evaluate customer service, operations, merchandising, product quality and, in special cases, employee integrity.

Mystery shopping is also known as

- Secret shopping
- Mystery customers
- Spotters
- Anonymous audits
- Virtual customers
- Employee evaluations
- Performance audits
- Telephone checks

Web site: One of many Mystery Shopping companies is http://www.azsecretshops.com.

The Mystery Shopping Providers Association (MSPA) says it is the largest professional trade association dedicated to improving service quality using anonymous resources: http://www.mysteryshop.org.

You can also survey your tenants directly each year to determine the extent of their satisfaction or dissatisfaction with the property.

Comparative Market Analysis

Renting units is a critical function of property management that must be done extremely well. It is not an easy task, because it requires you to constantly keep track of the market to understand the trends in vacancies in your community and what the competition is doing in terms of rents, concessions, and incentives. To begin, you should create a rental survey, or what is known as a comparative market analysis (CMA). You or your on-site manager must review competing properties regularly and log that information into the CMA (see Figure 9.1).

Property Management

Community Name	Grove Apts.	Sunset Apts.	The Cambridge	The Shelby
Phone				
Contact				
Address				
Number of units				
Year built				
Studios				
1 bed/1 bath - SF and rental rate				
2 bed/1 bath - SF and rental rate				
2 bed/2 bath - SF and rental rate				
3 bed/2 bath - SF and rental rate				
3 bed/3 bath - SF and rental rate				
Application fee				
Administration fee				
Security deposit studio				
Security deposit 1/1				
Security deposit 2/1				
Security deposit 2/2				
Security deposit 3/2				
Security deposit 3/3				
Pet deposit or fee				
Accept large pets				
Pet rents				
Pool, tennis, or basketball court				
Laundry facilities				
Cost of laundry cycle				
Washer/dryer in-unit hookups				
Clubhouse				
Gym				
Playground				
Water included				
Cable included				
Section 8				
Move-in specials				
Occupancy				
Last remodeled				
Rent includes anything else				
Notes				

Figure 9.1   Comparative market analysis

The on-site managers or leasing agents must track all the property's rental activity by maintaining a log of all prospective tenants' inquiries, property tours, tenant feedback, and the results of any follow-up discussions.

Finding New Tenants

Here are some examples of ways to target prospective tenants and fill vacancies:

- *Signage.* Place a "For Rent" sign at the property to attract people who drive or walk by it.
- *Newspaper.* Place a rental ad in your local newspaper. Include information about the unit(s), its address, the asking rent, the date of availability, and your contact information. If there are several papers in your city, try all of them until you determine which one works best for your specific purposes.
- *Internet.* Place an ad on an Internet rental site such as Craigslist, Apartments.com, or Rent.com. Also, consider more narrowly focused niche sites such as internhousing.com or nursehousing.com.
- *Flyers.* Place flyers describing your rental property on bulletin boards in local grocery stores, coffee shops, businesses, churches, gyms, and community centers. Blanket a five-mile radius around your property with flyers.

APARTMENTS FOR RENT

1 & 2 bedrooms available now
ONLY $500 security deposit
Starting at $999

Cambridge Heights Apartments
1515 Main Street
Cambridge, MA
www.cambridgeheightsapt.com

Call Today
555-555-5555

- *Referral program.* Inform your current tenants about the units that are available, and establish a tenant referral program. Pay your existing tenants if they introduce you to new tenants. Individuals referred by existing tenants are a wonderful source of new tenants.

Accept referrals only from good tenants who are current on their own rent. Avoid paying any referral fees until the new tenant has paid the rent on time for three consecutive months.

Note: Advertising Incentives Marketing (AIM) offers a tenant retention and attraction program to property owners and management companies. It offers cruise vacation certificates valued at more than $1,500 for a cost of only $169. You can promote these certificates as an effective incentive for referrals.

- *Word of mouth.* Have your property manager, maintenance staff, vendors, and other such people tell their friends and business associates about the availability of units.
- *Open house.* Invite the community to your property, and showcase your rental property to neighbors.
- *Brokers.* You may compensate brokers a half or a full month's rent if they help you fill vacant units. Establish an open line of communication with local brokers, and be sure they realize that they will earn a finder's fee if they help you fill your vacancies.
- *Foreclosure market.* Many homeowners will, unfortunately, lose their homes to foreclosure. However, those homeowners will also be returning to the rental market in droves, and they will be a new source of tenants for many years to come.

Leasing Agents

Be sure to ask every person who calls the office how he heard about the property. A great deal of time, energy, and money goes into creating advertising and outreach campaigns designed to generate phone calls to leasing offices. However, leasing agents also must do their job in renting units or all of your marketing efforts will result in very few leases.

When it comes to filling vacancies, you could spend thousands of dollars in advertising each month but never achieve your objectives if your leasing agents aren't highly skilled at getting leases signed.

Leasing agents must qualify callers and set appointments to show units. They must obtain the callers' names and their complete contact information so that the agent can follow up with each caller.

Most leasing agents should convert 40 to 50 percent of callers into appointments. The conversations that leasing agents have with prospective tenants can mean the difference between a property with 70 percent occupancy and one with 95 percent occupancy.

Make sure your agents ask the following on each call:

1. The caller's name, phone number, and e-mail address.
2. When does the prospect need the apartment?
3. How did the caller hear about the apartment?
4. What is the caller's budget?
5. What kind of apartment does the person need?
6. When can the caller visit the property and tour a unit?

All calls *should* be recorded, reviewed, and logged.

Screening Tenants

Always, always, *always* screen prospective tenants. Good tenants pay their rent on time, take care of the property, and create additional value because they attract other good tenants. The most costly expenses you'll encounter in this business are those associated with vacancies, evictions, property damage, and unit turnover. Make the following screening techniques part of your overall plan to ensure that an applicant will be a good tenant:

1. *Application fee.* A nominal fee that covers the cost of obtaining a credit and criminal report is reasonable and provides a safeguard for all the tenants. If a prospective tenant objects to this fee, you should reject his application.
2. *Identification.* A copy of the applicant's driver's license with his name and address should be obtained. You'll also need the applicant's social security number and another form of ID that corroborates the information on the driver's license. If a prospective tenant prefers to hide his identity, you should not rent to him.

Property Management

3. *Application.* If the applicant doesn't enter all the information called for on the application, you should request that he answer every question before he leaves. Check that all of the information is legible. Call all the references: personal, employment, and both current and previous landlords. The applicant's references should speak highly of him. If a previous landlord claims that the applicant didn't pay his rent and was evicted, you should expect that he will do the same to you. Once again, if people are hesitant to provide any information that is being requested or if their references can't be verified, a red flag should be raised.

4. *Credit check.* After completing these first three steps, you must check an applicant's credit history. If the credit rating falls below your minimum threshold, you must reject the tenant. Your standards must be the same for all of your prospective tenants.

5. *Criminal check.* If an applicant has a criminal record, it might be wise to reject his application.

Web sites: The following Web sites are online services that provide credit and criminal verification for owners of rental properties:

http://www.citicredit.net
http://www.e-renter.com
http://www.youcheckcredit.com
http://on-site.com
http://www.tenantalert.com
http://www.tenantverification.com
http://www.simplescreening.com
http://www.creditlink.com

RentBureau collects rental payment histories nationwide and stores the data in a proprietary database. The company provides this information for a fee to property managers as part of their screening process.

Web site: http://rentbureau.com.

Discrimination

Never—repeat, *never*—discriminate in this business! Leasing agents and property owners can decide whom to rent to based on objective criteria that are applied equally to every prospective tenant. These criteria include employment status, creditworthiness, ability to pay rent, personal references, and the existence of a criminal record. For example, if a person has a poor track record of paying rent, you can deny his application.

Unfortunately, discrimination takes place all over the country, whether you're in Boston, Miami, Chicago, or Los Angeles. The federal Fair Housing Act bans discrimination based on race, disability, national origin, sex, skin color, religion, or whether a person has children. Credit, references, criminal records, and the ability to pay rent should be the deciding factors when deciding to approve a tenant's application, as these are both legal and nondiscriminatory. Nevertheless, housing discrimination complaints appear to be on the rise. The number of discrimination complaints recorded by the Department of Housing and Urban Development increased from 8,097 in 2003 to 10,328 in 2006.

Accepting a tenant who passes your screening is basic. However, rejecting an applicant is significantly more challenging. Here are some tips for protecting yourself:

1. Establish rental criteria and attach them to every rental application. Every applicant should know your specific requirements.
2. Do not modify or alter your rental criteria. For example, if your rule is that everyone you accept must have a credit score of 600 or higher, you must abide by this rule and not rent to a well-mannered prospect with a score of 590.
3. If you're going to decline an applicant, be prepared to state why—and use a standard form to notify him of your decision.
4. Maintain copies of all the documents used and any notes taken during the application process.

Web sites: For more information on housing discrimination, see

U.S. Department of Housing and Urban Development: www.hud.gov
National Fair Housing Alliance: www.nationalfairhousing.org

Keeping Tenants Satisfied

Because your tenants are the backbone of your business, they must remain your top priority at all times. Respond to maintenance and service calls as quickly as possible. Try to routinely follow up on any legitimate tenant concern or request within 24 hours. Also, forward any notices informing tenants of changes in policies, future maintenance projects or any other news regarding the property well in advance. Notices can be communicated to tenants by posting the information in the common areas or the management office or by sending individuals an e-mail or a letter. Forging a trusted relationship between the on-site manager and your tenants is also important. You want to encourage fluid communication between the tenants and the management office. Regularly scheduled yet informal meetings can help to identify problems. These meetings enable tenants to express their concerns about the property and to help find solutions to problems.

Note: Given that tenants rarely call about leaking toilets but will call immediately when a toilet isn't working, I instruct my property managers to install a product called the Fluid Master with leak prevention in every bathroom. A leaking toilet can waste up to 200 gallons a day and can cost you thousands of dollars each month. For about $9, the Fluid Master shuts off the water to a leaking toilet, thereby prompting the tenant to call maintenance if he wants to use the toilet again.

Web site: www.fluidmaster.com.

Departing Tenants

To be successful in this line of work, you must service your customers extremely well. Your tenants are your customers. One way to better understand how well you have served them is to conduct exit interviews when they leave your property. These reports will highlight any issues or problems that could have been a deciding factor in their decision to find another home.

Tenant Exit Interview

Date _____ Property _____

Name of tenant: _____

Length of tenancy: _____ Type of unit: _____

Forwarding address and telephone number:

_____

Stated reason for moving: *(Include details such as information about new location, size, rent, lease terms, purchased property, and so on)*

_____

_____

_____

Comments/suggestions: *(How could we have served the tenant better?)*

_____

_____

_____

Type of interview: _____ In person _____ Telephone

Completed by: _____

Rent-Ready Apartments

When a tenant vacates a unit, the apartment needs to be cleaned and painted, and anything that is broken needs to be fixed. After the completion of this work, a unit is ready to be toured by prospective tenants. A unit that's available to be seen by potential renters is referred to as a "rent-ready" unit.

All of the work associated with making a unit rent-ready should not take more than a week unless extensive repairs are required. The manager should inspect the vacant unit once a tenant moves out as well as during and after cleaning. Units that are clean, newly painted and, by all means, smelling good will rent much faster. Your goal is to rent the unit as quickly as possible, so make sure it shows well.

The airline industry knows that when its planes aren't in the air, they aren't generating revenue. When they are sitting idle on the tarmac, require repairs, or for whatever reason are not transporting passengers, they are not maximizing their economic potential. Lawyers also understand this concept quite well. They have only so many hours each day, so they must bill as many of them as possible. Apartment building owners also realize that vacant units are the equivalent of planes sitting on tarmacs or lawyers who take three-hour lunches without billing a client. If you have apartments that aren't rented, they are losing money every day.

Owner Involvement

All investors in apartment buildings need to be involved. You must read your monthly financial reports. You must inspect the property regularly. You must make sure that you and your property manager are on the same page and approve a management plan each year. You must reinvest enough money into the property to keep it competitive in the marketplace. No property will operate to its full potential without constant supervision from the owner.

Absentee owners should expect problems and must implement fail-safe strategies to avoid complete failure. After all, no one will care as much about your investments as you do. You are at a distinct disadvantage if you are unable to tour your investments periodically. If you decide to acquire properties outside of your immediate area, you still need to be actively involved. Try to visit your properties as often as possible. In fact, it's best if you don't inform your property managers when you plan to visit. This way, they are always kept on the alert. Unless a property manager has consistently performed well for you in the past, he should *not* be trusted 100 percent—he must earn your trust.

Reporting

At the beginning of each month, your property manager should prepare a management report for each of your buildings. Because rent is due by the first of the month and is late by the third (depending on your rules, it could be the fourth or fifth), management reports should be e-mailed to the owners no later than the fifteenth. These reports detail all rents received and expenses paid for the previous month. They also should include the following:

1. An income statement showing the gross revenue and operating expenses for the month and year
2. A comparison of the monthly income and operating expenses with the budgeted amounts for the month and year
3. Copies of all invoices paid
4. A summary of maintenance activity, delinquent rents, and new and expiring leases and a list of any other problems or management concerns, along with suggestions for how management intends to resolve each problem

Sophisticated management software is available that helps managers update everything from rent rolls to operating expenses to invoices paid. The leading property management software companies are

- Yardi: http://yardi.com
- Rent Manager: http://www.rentmanager.com
- MRI: http://www.realestate.intuit.com/products
- On-Site: http://on-site.com/

According to the National Multi Housing Council, as much as 2 to 5 percent of rental revenue is lost each year because of residents who

- Leave apartments without giving notice.
- Write checks on accounts with insufficient funds.
- Are evicted.
- Vacate suddenly, leaving their apartments damaged.

In the $115 billion apartment industry, that amounts to $2 to $5 billion that is owed and could be recovered annually. Property management software helps to keep track of all of these issues and is certainly a required tool for all professional management companies.

Collection of Rents and Delinquency

Never, ever allow your managers to collect rent in cash. Violation of this guideline will cost you money. All collected rents must be deposited immediately, and proof of the rental payment must be recorded. If the rent is not received on time, a notice to the tenant must be sent immediately. If the tenant has not paid the rent by the fifteenth of the month, you should commence the eviction process if you are unable to work out a payment plan with the tenant. However, you can bend the rules from time to time: If, for example, you have an otherwise good tenant who is experiencing a difficult month financially, by all means you should make an exception.

Renter Demographics

Between now and 2015, the number of renter households will increase by 1.8 million, according to Harvard's Joint Center for Housing Studies. National Multi Housing Council data also show that minorities will be responsible for much of the gain and eventually will account for a majority of all renter households. The number of Hispanic renters will nearly double by 2020. The median age of the Latino population is 26 compared to the U.S. population's average age of about 36. The echo boomers are the other group that will drive rental demand. Hispanics want larger apartments because they typically house multiple generations under one roof, but echo boomers want high-tech offerings such as Internet access, and most prefer to be close to shopping, cultural, and entertainment centers.

The U.S. 2007 generational breakdown as a percentage of the total population is

- Baby boomers = 38 percent
- Gen X = 22 percent
- Echo boomers = 12 percent

However, when analyzing these groups as apartment residents, echo boomers take a commanding lead:

- Baby boomers = 26 percent
- Gen X = 25 percent
- Echo boomers = 29 percent

Who Rents?

- One-third of all U.S. households.
- More than 80 percent of all households aged 25 or under and 66 percent of those aged 25 to 29.
- Some 4.1 million households from individuals aged 65 and older.
- About 60 percent of households who moved because of divorce or separation.
- Between now and 2020, the number of Hispanic renters will nearly double.

Population Trends

According to multifamily housing professionals, the 10 most likely locations for future population growth are

1. Phoenix, Arizona
2. Los Angeles, California
3. Las Vegas, Nevada

4. Houston, Texas
5. Orange County, California
6. Miami, Florida
7. Riverside County, California
8. Fort Lauderdale, Florida
9. Dallas, Texas
10. San Diego, California

The 10 most likely locations for future population loss are

1. Baltimore, Maryland
2. Syracuse, New York
3. Utica-Rome, New York
4. Cayuga County, New York
5. Jamestown, New York
6. Pittsburgh, Pennsylvania
7. Johnstown, Pennsylvania
8. New Orleans, Louisiana
9. Houma, Louisiana
10. St. Bernard, Louisiana

Chapter Summary

- The very best property owners know that the profitability of their rental business is determined to a large extent by the way their properties are managed. Good tenant selection, owner involvement, and competent managers make all the difference in the world.
- If you are new to the rental property business, try managing your own properties for a while. The experience you'll gain will be extremely valuable to you as a real estate investor.
- After you've gained some experience, hire a competent management company or property manager to assist you with the day-to-day operations.
- Filling vacancies is of the utmost importance. Make sure that you and your management team make this a priority.

- Train your leasing agents and be sure they are effective in converting inbound calls to on-site tours to leases.
- The renters of tomorrow are younger and Hispanic. Make sure that you understand what they want or you'll lose prospective tenants to the competition.

10

Exit Strategy and Disposition

*99 percent of the failures come from people who
have the habit of making excuses.*
—George Washington Carver

What You're About to Learn

- Market trends
- Real estate indices
- Economic signals
- When to sell
- Timing the market for dispositions
- Liquidity events
- Brokers in sales transactions
- Disposition strategy
- Generational wealth

Investing in Apartment Buildings

arcel Arsenault is one of the shrewdest real estate investors in the country. I've had the privilege of working with him, and I've witnessed firsthand how meticulous he and his team are in underwriting, analyzing, and understanding real estate opportunities. Most other institutional investors tend to be overly rigid in their acquisition and disposition strategy, but he takes an extremely entrepreneurial approach to investing. A molecular biologist by training, he made his first million by founding a yogurt business that he eventually sold to Beatrice Foods. He parlayed those profits into a real estate company that today manages a portfolio of assets in excess of $200 million. He says, "In troubled times, cash is king. History shows us that real estate moves in cycles. We know cycles, and we know an opportunity when we see it. It's an imperfect science—you can predict the seasons, but you can't predict every day's weather. We're [in the business of] predicting seasons!"

The Denver Business Journal recently wrote about Mr. Arsenault's unique vision for real estate investing: "He purchased distressed commercial real estate, nurtured it to health, and resold it at a higher market value in the 1980s . . . diversifying his portfolio in the 1990s—purchasing what he calls 'boring but stable' properties, maximizing cash flow, and strengthening the quality of its tenant base."

To understand market cycles the way Marcel does, you must be knowledgeable about the prevailing conditions in the multifamily housing market while having the foresight to know what's to come beyond the horizon. To begin predicting real estate trends, however, you must develop a keen understanding of the industry's most influential economic signals:

- Employment growth
- Vacancy rates
- Interest rates
- Rental rates
- Mortgage rates
- Consumer confidence
- Inflation rate
- Apartment mortgage delinquency rates

- Housing affordability
- Retail sales (yes, even retail sales!)

> *Defined:* Economic indicators are statistics that are used to forecast financial and economic trends.

Given the complex nature of the real estate industry, it is extremely helpful to search for trends that indicate the direction in which the market is moving. Here are some of the most important ones:

1. *Population.* A growing population means greater demand for housing. Greater demand usually results in higher rents and lower vacancy rates.
2. *Rental rates.* Are the rents in your area going up or down? Are concessions being made? If so, how much are landlords offering as incentives to entice prospective tenants to sign leases, and what's the effective rent?
3. *Interest rates.* Whether you're a renter, a buyer, or a seller, interest rates affect the cost of obtaining capital. Higher interest rates make it more difficult for families to buy homes and thus can limit them to renting. However, higher rates also make it more costly for investors to finance the acquisition of new apartment buildings or to sell to prospective buyers.
4. *Employment.* Rising local employment and job growth are good signs for the rental business. When the rate of employment increases, higher population growth, lower vacancy rates, higher rents, and fewer concessions follow. The opposite is true when unemployment is increasing.
5. *New home starts.* More new units create additional housing supply, which can affect the demand for rentals dramatically. Check with the local homebuilders' association, local chamber of commerce, town hall, or economic development office about construction permits, housing completions, and new home starts.

Investing in Apartment Buildings

There are numerous other indicators that are just as compelling, albeit less scientific—and that probably are not found in the business section of your local paper.

For instance, contact a moving company's local facility manager to determine whether more people are moving out of the area than are moving in. I toured one of the PODS (Portable On Demand Storage—www.pods.com) facilities and was told by the manager that 70 percent of his business was heading out of the state rather than into the state. Population declines negatively affect occupancy rates by reducing the demand for housing.

Also, talk with your local builders to determine whether they are experiencing any changes in the market. My brother-in-law works for a building supply company, and he noticed a downward trend in sales much earlier than the papers began writing stories about the decline in housing demand.

One of my friends is a private wealth manager at UBS, a financial services firm. When he told me that five real estate developers had opened accounts with him during a two-month span, I most certainly took note. This information alone wasn't necessarily newsworthy, but then he mentioned that the developers had sold 100 percent of their real estate holdings and wanted to reinvest the proceeds in bonds. After gathering this information from the moving company, my brother-in-law, and my friend at UBS, I was confident that things were changing in early 2006; I didn't need to be convinced by the *Wall Street Journal* that the residential real estate market was experiencing a major adjustment.

Be aware of your environment (keep your eyes and ears to the ground, so to speak) so that you can better predict what the future holds and modify your strategy accordingly. Although I could discuss this topic ad nauseam, I won't. However, you should know that every market cycle has a critical inflection point when conditions either change for the better or change for the worse. Notice the signs of a changing market and avoid being taken by surprise.

Market Timing

Most of the prodigiously successful real estate investors I know bought during down cycles and sold at the top of the market. This buy-low, sell-high mentality has, indeed, created great fortunes. Nevertheless, my basic real estate philosophy remains the same:

- Never try to time the market.
- Emphasize buying value regardless of the prevailing market conditions, but certainly take advantage of down cycles.
- Buy properties that can generate positive cash flow in the near term and outstanding returns in the long term.
- Acquire properties from motivated sellers and place them under good, aggressive management with the goal of improving their net operating income (NOI).
- Focus on locations with high barriers to entry, but always concentrate on a specific farm area regardless of where you decide to buy.
- Dispose of a property when it attains its target NOI and the returns you desire can be achieved. You'll never go broke selling for a profit!
- Buy for the long term, but be prepared to sell when it makes good financial sense.
- Develop multiple exit strategies before buying a property.
- Run the numbers for the worst-case scenario, and if they still work, then by all means proceed.

Attempting to predict the ebb and flow of the market with great precision can be difficult. Concentrate on growing NOI and cash flow through the use of intense management, while taking advantage of market cycles, and you will do just fine.

U.S. MULTIFAMILY HOUSING MARKET STRENGTH FORECAST

Top Markets 2008–2012*

United States	Overall Score*	Rank
Los Angeles, California	65.0	1
Washington, D.C.	54.9	2
Orange County, California	53.5	3
San Diego, California	52.4	4
Oakland/East Bay, California	52.1	5
Dallas/Fort Worth, Texas	47.9	6
New Jersey	45.9	7
San Jose, California	45.8	8
New York City	44.0	9

*Markets were ranked from 0 to 100 against 13 property, economic and demographic variables.
SOURCE: Grubb & Ellis Company.

Disposition

Some investors steadfastly believe that one never should sell a property. They say, "You should hold on to every asset until the day you die!" Their argument is that finding, negotiating for, financing, closing on, managing, improving, and maintaining an apartment building is too challenging to then sell the building. "Why on earth would you ever want to sell? Hold on to it for dear life and let your children inherit it."

Other investors, myself included, subscribe to a different investment philosophy. Investors should continually reevaluate their portfolio, and if the sale of a property can achieve the return on capital that you require, or if there's an alternative investment opportunity that could generate higher returns with the proceeds from the sale of a currently owned asset, then by all means, you should consider selling.

In general, when you dispose of a property, it's typically beneficial to sell only when you really don't have to. In other words, don't be one of those motivated sellers who are forced to sell at steep discounts because they need the money. You only want to buy from motivated sellers; you don't want to be one of them.

If you're eager to sell because of poor health, financial difficulties, or other personal circumstances, you should be prepared for diminished returns or even a loss. Exiting from the real estate you own is an important business decision that takes careful analysis and thoughtful consideration.

Brokers

After you've made the decision to sell, you can either attempt to dispose of the property on your own or select an experienced broker who has a proven track record and a large Rolodex. A good broker has a positive, never-give-up attitude. At times, it might seem that a deal is going to crumble or that the two parties will never agree on terms or price, but a competent, experienced broker will find a way to bridge the gap. The techniques and strategies needed to consummate a deal are not learned overnight. Outstanding brokerage skills come only with experience and time. The negotiations can become extremely emotional and even volatile at times. A good broker will overcome these conflicts with workable solutions and sound advice.

Lesson learned: I once was selling a large apartment complex and had a buyer who was interested in the property but who had difficulty finding a lender to fund the project. We were at the eleventh hour in the deal when, moments before it was about to implode, my Realtor introduced the buyer to a local lender (with whom she had worked in the past). To make a long story short, the buyer was able to secure the loan from this particular lender, and it resulted in an immediate sale. I'm confident that the sale might not have taken place without this broker. Don't undervalue the contribution that a competent and experienced real estate broker can bring to each transaction.

Obtain a written marketing plan before you commit to an exclusive listing. Know how your Realtor is going to actively market your property. Otherwise, he will just list it on LoopNet and field phone calls. You should ask about the broker's plans to advertise in or to

- Local newspapers
- Local real estate investor associations
- Personal and companywide databases of prospective investors
- A company network
- Other property owners in the area

I want a broker who will exhaust every possibility in finding the highest bidder and the most qualified buyer for my property.

Flexibility is important as well. If you and the buyer can't agree on price, you might ask the broker(s) to consider reducing their commission(s) to bridge the chasm between your lowest acceptable price and the buyer's offer.

Liquidity Event

A significant liquidity event is an exit strategy that all aspiring business tycoons aim to achieve at least once in a lifetime. A liquidity event occurs when, for example, an executive liquidates his shares in a company, an entrepreneur sells the company he founded, or a real estate entrepreneur disposes of properties in which he has an equity stake. The conversion of equity into cash is a liquidity event. Such an event can lead to great fortunes. Although the run-up to a liquidity event may have taken years or even decades, this one financial event can create great wealth for the stakeholders. In fact, the number of millionaire households has more than doubled during the past decade, and the heads of many of these households undoubtedly participated in a liquidity event of one kind or another.

- The number of millionaire households in 1995 was 3.7 million.
- The number of millionaire households in 1998 was 5.4 million.
- The number of millionaire households in 2004 was 9 million.

Generational Wealth

Generational wealth is wealth that is passed on to your heirs upon your death. It becomes generational when, for example, your children use the money they inherited from you to generate additional wealth and pass it on to their heirs, who then repeat the process over and over again. I mention generational wealth here because it's unlikely that you'll ever be able to generate enough momentum with earned income alone to pass on a significant amount of wealth to your heirs. Portfolio and/or passive income (the kind, for example, that the ex-CEO of Lycos received or that Marcel Arsenault have created with real estate) will be required for such a wealth transfer. If you aren't willing to spend decades climbing the corporate ladder until the day you're eventually eligible for a CEO position, I recommend being the founder of your own business or investing in real estate as realistic means for significant wealth creation.

> *Lesson learned:* To accumulate wealth, investment in assets is required, and consumption, at least for the short term, must be sacrificed. In other words, don't buy that 65-foot yacht. Instead, invest that money in an apartment building or other appreciating asset so that one day you truly can afford to buy those luxury items.

Chapter Summary

- To be an astute investor, you should track the various indices that influence real estate supply, demand, and prices: employment, population growth, housing affordability, interest rates, housing starts, vacancy rates, and other such data.
- Be alert to any changes in your area, and anticipate future market trends rather than fall victim to them.
- Never try to time the market, but certainly take advantage of market cycles.
- Emphasize buying value regardless of the prevailing market conditions.

Investing in Apartment Buildings

- Buy properties that can generate cash flow in the near term.
- Buy properties from motivated sellers. Avoid becoming a motivated seller.
- Employ aggressive management practices that will result in dramatic improvements in the property's NOI.
- Dispose of the property when it attains its target NOI and you are able to achieve your desired rate of return on the capital invested.
- Buy for the long term, but be prepared to sell when it makes sense.
- If you're eager to sell because of poor health, financial difficulties, or other personal circumstances, you should be prepared for diminished returns or even a loss.
- Don't underestimate the value of a good broker when selling.

11

Beyond Apartment Buildings

You have to learn the rules of the game. And
then you have to play better than anyone else.
—ALBERT EINSTEIN

What You're About to Learn

- Asset classes other than multifamily housing
- Mixed-use properties
- Retail opportunities
- Brokering retail deals
- Gaining experience in retail before investing in it
- Retail condos
- How to master multifamily, then expand your horizons

Investing in Apartment Buildings

Income-producing property is acquired (or in some cases developed) so that the investor can generate an income stream by leasing the space in exchange for rent. As discussed, income-producing property can be classified as residential or commercial. Buying, renting, and selling multifamily residential housing is just one option among many in the real estate industry. In addition to multifamily residential properties, you also could explore the following types of commercial property:

- Office buildings
- Industrial properties
- Retail properties
- Hotel/lodging/hospitality/resort properties

Office buildings, for example, are places of business where companies lease space for their employees to perform their work. Office buildings can be found in your town's central business district (CBD) and in other locations zoned for office use.

An example of an industrial property is a warehouse where products are stored or a factory where they are assembled or manufactured. Industrial properties are often found in proximity to airports because parts can be transported to the site more readily, and finished products can be sent to other destinations quickly and efficiently. For instance, 75 percent of all flowers imported into the United States are shipped to Miami from Latin America. They are stored in very large industrial warehouses and are processed, packaged, and forwarded (typically by plane to expedite delivery) to destinations throughout the country.

Retail properties include, for example, all of the strip malls and shopping centers that you pass on your way to work or school each day. Retail properties are places of business where companies sell their products or services to the general public. Examples of retail locations include grocery stores, fast-food outlets, cell phone stores, restaurants, and pharmacies. These stores can be found in an indoor or outdoor shopping center, a strip mall, or their own stand-alone building.

Finally, hotels (hospitality/resort properties) are places where individuals rent rooms for a specified period of time. Widely known brands

Beyond Apartment Buildings

include Hilton, Marriott, Best Western, Four Seasons, Ritz-Carlton, and Sheraton.

Mixed-use properties consist of more than one of the aforementioned asset types. An example of a mixed-use property is an apartment or office building with a retail component on the ground level.

If you are an active investor in multifamily properties, but you want to explore investing in different asset types to broaden your real estate expertise, you should consider buying an apartment building with a retail component on the ground level. A mixed-use property such as this can be a very good way of gaining experience with another asset class while still maintaining your emphasis on what you know and do best.

A good friend of mine acquired an eight-unit building in the heart of Boston with two apartments on each of the second, third, and fourth floors, along with two retail units on the ground floor. Because the zoning permitted retail/office use, he was able to generate far superior rents from the first-floor units by leasing them as retail space rather than converting them to apartments. He negotiated favorable leases for both retail units, and not only did he maximize the property's net operating income, but he also was able to learn more about a new asset class (including how to manage companies rather than families) while not straying too far from his expertise with multifamily properties.

Another way of gaining more experience with retail assets is to broker space to companies that are actively searching in your market. After seven years in the multifamily industry, I began to develop a keen interest in retail. I realized, however, that the fundamentals of the retail business were foreign to me and that I would have to learn them if I was serious about venturing into a new asset class. NNN (triple net), gross and percentage leases, CAM (common area maintenance), daily car counts, corner lots at signalized intersections, end caps, outparcels, TI money, and parking ratios were terms that I didn't fully understand.

Every asset type has its own unique complexities, jargon, and terminology, but I was determined to learn this new business, so I decided that brokering a deal or two while taking a few more classes and reading several books on commercial real estate was the best way for me to gain the expertise that I needed before making a retail purchase for my own portfolio. While taking a commercial real estate class, I met an individual who worked for the real estate division of a major retailer. I asked if she would introduce me to the director of real estate, who was responsible for site locations. This chain has nearly 30,000 stores in more than 86 countries, so I figured I could learn a lot about the retail business if I aligned myself with this organization. I eventually met the person in charge, and he reluctantly gave me an opportunity to help. My timing must have been good, since they needed to open about 100 new stores and required assistance in finding suitable locations. The director was a 72-year-old expert in the retail business. He had owned restaurants in several states, had worked in the real estate department at Burger King, and had been at his current position for more than a decade. More important, he was patient, a good teacher, and willing to show me how the retail business worked. We spent months driving around neighborhoods, visiting shopping centers, and touring retail sites. He would explain why a certain location would or would not work. He introduced me to new concepts such as the importance of store visibility, high car counts, good demographics, signage, tenant improvement allowances, and much, much more. He showed me how to negotiate a retail contract and what to include in the final agreement. To make a long story short, I learned retail by finding a mentor and contributing value to his initiatives. Perhaps this is an option for you to explore as well.

If you are on the "lease" side (i.e., tenant rep), representing national chain stores in your local community, you will be contacting shopping center owners to determine whether they have available space to rent to your clients. This is your opportunity to meet more property owners and help fill vacancies in their retail properties. It's also an opportunity to learn from them while earning valuable commission checks from the national retailers you represent. Eventually, you might purchase one of their shopping centers, so be sure to nurture these relationships and always conduct your business transactions with the highest standards of ethics and professionalism.

Of course, you don't need to work with a national retailer to gain more knowledge in another sector. You could simply introduce yourself to the owner of a strip mall and ask whether he would consider buying more properties. Schedule a meeting with the owner to evaluate his specific needs, budget, time schedule, and acquisition criteria. After the meeting, you can start searching for suitable retail centers that he could potentially acquire. During the process, you'll learn more about the business without risking your own capital—until, of course, you are ready to do so.

I highly recommend that you obtain a real estate license so that you can gain more expertise about the industry while also being compensated for your efforts. Your client will not be able to legally pay you a commission unless you're licensed in the state in which you are conducting business. Moreover, you should place your license with a real estate firm that is active in the retail marketplace. Surrounding yourself with professionals who are dedicated to a particular asset class will prove beneficial one day.

Retail Condos

I've been reading a lot about retail condos lately. I've also been speaking with developers of retail space to try to better understand the viability of a business model based on unit sales. Initially, I concluded that national retailers would not buy this type of space because they don't want real estate debt on their books. For instance, many national chains do not own a single one of their stores. Instead, they sign leases for up to 20 years for each location. Also, small mom-and-pop retailers just can't afford to buy their retail space because, in most places, the benefits of renting rather than buying are so great that they preclude most retailers from even considering buying. However, times are changing, and retailers are now much more receptive to the notion of buying their space.

Dan Fasulo, managing director of Real Capital Analytics, said recently, "Retail condos are not a major nationwide phenomenon yet, but the sales in this sector are growing at an impressive rate."

Investing in Apartment Buildings

Although the recording of retail condo sales only recently started in 2003, they have had an impressive sales trajectory since that time:

2003	$45 million
2004	$625 million
2005	$650 million
2006	$862 million
2007	$250 million
	(through August)

SOURCE: *National Real Estate Investor*, November 2007.

With interest rates low, some retailers have concluded they can buy their space for no more than it would cost them to rent it, while also receiving the benefits of ownership, such as property appreciation, equity buildup, and tax write-offs.

As with apartments, if you own a shopping center and can't sell the units (similar to condos in an apartment building), you always can go back to renting them—a problem that most condo converters are experiencing these days. The similarities between multifamily housing and retail make the redeployment of your capital into this new asset class the most logical next step.

There are about 30 real estate billionaires in the United States today. However, the common denominator among all of them is that they've built prodigious portfolios that include more than one category of real estate asset.

I'm sure a few of these billionaires started with a few rentals in economically depressed parts of their own hometowns. They succeeded by specializing in one asset class, then branching out when the time was right.

If you want to grow your real estate holdings, you should first concentrate on a core asset class in a specific area and become very good at it before venturing out into other assets. But you also should make a habit of educating yourself and continually learning about other real estate assets so that, when an opportunity presents itself, you'll be prepared to move forward.

Chapter Summary

- Types of real estate assets include multifamily, retail, office, industrial, and hotel/lodging properties.
- Mixed-use properties have two or more real estate asset types in one building.
- If you want to learn another asset class besides multifamily, retail tends to be the most similar.
- There are many ways to learn retail before you actually invest in this asset class. For example, you could work for a retailer or owner of a shopping center.
- Retail condos may offer above-average returns in the future.
- Master multifamily properties before moving on to other asset classes.

12

Success

Failure is a precondition to success.
—ROBERT FRANK

*One of the fundamental requirements of being
an entrepreneur is being naive.*
—ROBERT FRANK

*In an economy driven more than ever by
competition and innovation, the people who
succeed tend to be those who thrive on risk,
reinvention and brutal hours.*
—ROBERT FRANK

*If you look back through the annals of history,
the truly successful people have been those who
have been most adept at managing change.*
—SAM ZELL

Look at a man in the midst of doubt and danger,
and you will learn in his hour of adversity what
he really is.

—ROMAN POET

Failure is only an opportunity to begin again
more intelligently.

—HENRY FORD

Success is liking yourself, liking what you do,
and liking how you do it.

—MAYA ANGELOU

What You're About to Learn

- Why "never giving up" is the mantra of all successful investors
- The law of attraction
- Inequities of the classes
- The proletariat versus the bourgeoisie
- Income diversification plan

Jim Randel, a good friend of mine and the author of *Confessions of a Real Estate Entrepreneur*, commented to a group of budding real estate investors, "I'm an Ivy League-educated attorney. I've been taught by some of the finest professors this country has to offer. Do you know what that amounts to in the real estate industry? Absolutely nothing! A big fat zero! To succeed in the game of real estate entrepreneurship, you must be smart, hungry, and never give up! Don't let your lack of education, pedigree, or daddy's money serve as a deterrent to realizing your dreams."

Success

Have you ever read a Dr. Seuss book? Well, Theodor Seuss wrote more than 64 books and taught several generations of children that learning to read could be fun. He sold more than 400 million books; they were translated into 20 languages, and three were made into blockbuster films (*The Grinch*, *The Cat in the Hat*, and *Horton Hears a Who!*). In 1984 Dr. Seuss won a Pulitzer Prize. But the statistic that most interested me was that 27 publishers rejected his first book. This is a man who never accepted no as the final answer, a man who never, ever gave up.

I've received a lot of advice over the years; however, it seems that the very best advice (albeit very simple) has been to never give up. *Never, ever give up.* Find a way to do what others can't do, and you will succeed beyond your wildest imagination. Realizing that few things that are worthwhile are obtained easily and that perseverance is what sets successful investors apart from everyone else, the very best investors don't know how to give up. They don't let negativity permeate their thoughts. Instead, they allow the power of positive thinking to prevail.

The Law of Attraction

My wonderful wife introduced me to the law of attraction about a year ago. This law states that if you think about a positive outcome, you're likely to achieve it. In other words, you get what you think about. For instance, if you think positively about the desired results, you'll create an achievable and logical path to those results. The law of attraction is based on the principle that individuals can achieve their desires if their overwhelming thoughts, feelings, and actions are positively oriented toward achieving that outcome. It suggests that anyone has the ability to greatly influence his or her life by shifting his or her mindset. The principle stems from the belief that a person's emotions, actions, and thoughts (whether they are conscious or unconscious) attract corresponding positive and/or negative results. I suspect that most people who really excel in this world apply some variation of this law to their everyday lives.

Titans of American Industry

In July 2007, the *New York Times* offered an interesting historical perspective on the wealthiest Americans of all time. It presented the following list:

1. John D. Rockefeller: $192 billion
2. Cornelius Vanderbilt: $143 billion
3. John Jacob Astor: $116 billion
4. Stephen Girard: $83 billion
5. Bill Gates: $82 billion
6. Andrew Carnegie: $75 billion
7. A. T. Stewart: $70 billion
8. Frederick Weyerhaeuser: $68 billion
9. Jay Gould: $67 billion
10. Stephen Van Rensselaer: $64 billion
11. Marshall Field: $61 billion
12. Henry Ford: $54 billion
13. Sam Walton: $53 billion
14. Andrew Mellon: $48 billion
15. Richard Mellon: $48 billion
16. Warren Buffett: $46 billion

The common thread among all these individuals is that each of them generated a vast fortune through his entrepreneurial achievements. Rockefeller developed Standard Oil; Astor benefited from his New York real estate investments; Gates founded Microsoft; Field had department stores and Chicago real estate; Ford manufactured automobiles in Detroit; Buffett made investments through Berkshire Hathaway.

Admittedly, most of these men created their wealth during the Gilded Age, but their industries and the social status to which they were born differed dramatically. Moreover, each of them invented either a new way of doing something or a better or more efficient way of doing it. For example, Ford developed the mass production of automobiles by perfecting the assembly line and conveyor belt system. Gates took the MS-DOS operating system, made it user-friendly, and created a near monopoly on desktop computers. Marshall Field introduced the first retail exchange policy at his national chain of department stores, which set him apart from the competition.

When you examine each of these men's business stories in depth, you realize that not only were all of these titans of American industry innovators, but they ultimately managed to reach great heights of success by never giving up and always persevering, regardless of their personal circumstances, challenges, and humble beginnings.

Now, becoming a member of the über-rich plutocracy might not be a realistic goal or even one that you aspire to achieve; however, firmly establishing yourself among the middle or upper middle class (or better) most certainly is a noble objective that can have widespread implications for you, your family, and even your country. After all, if you suddenly fall from grace and find yourself in the lower class, you'll probably have to forfeit access to such amenities as good schools, comprehensive health insurance, and a safe environment in which to live and work—amenities that you've probably taken for granted. The overwhelming disadvantages associated with not being part of one of the "chosen" classes are sometimes quite subtle, but all too often, they are blatantly overt and grossly unfair.

Here are two examples.

Two Examples: New Orleans and the Titanic

When New Orleans was devastated by hurricane Katrina in August 2005, 1,464 people died as a result of this natural disaster, and thousands more were displaced from their homes. New Orleans was a city in which 27.9 percent of its residents lived below the poverty line, 67.3 percent of the residents were African American, and 27.3 percent of households didn't even own automobiles. The chasm revealed by these statistics became all too obvious when the nightly news aired footage of the 25,000 people who were forced to take shelter in the Superdome. People's plans for evacuation were strongly influenced by their income, access to information, and transportation. Low-income families' options for evacuation were limited. "Since the storm was at the end of the month and many low-income residents of New Orleans live from paycheck to paycheck, economic resources for evacuating were particularly scarce," wrote Elizabeth Fussell, a professor of sociology at Tulane University in "Leaving New Orleans," published by SSRC.

When the *Titanic* collided with an iceberg and sank on April 14, 1912, social class proved to be a key determinant of who survived and who perished. There were a total of 2,207 passengers and crew members on board; of these, 1,495 people died and 712 survived. Among the women, 3 percent of the first-class passengers drowned, compared to 16 percent of the second-class and 45 percent of the third-class passengers. All but one of the first-class passengers were able to abandon ship. However, all of the third-class passengers had been ordered at gunpoint to go below decks, and most of them died because of it.

The American Class Structure by Dennis Gilbert and Joseph Kahl summarizes the survivors by class:

- 324 total first-class passengers; 201 (or 62 percent) survived.
- 277 total second-class passengers; 118 (or 43 percent) survived.
- 708 total third-class passengers; 181 (or 25 percent) survived.
- 898 crew members; 212 (or 24 percent) survived.

Karl Marx

There's absolutely nothing wrong with being gainfully employed by someone else. In fact, since being self-employed, I've received more job offers than ever before. Some of these offers have piqued my interest and led me to reconsider being an entrepreneur. After all, why not let someone else assume all the financial risk? I can continue to do what I enjoy doing, but have the financial and administrative support needed to reach the next level of success. Everyone's goals, aspirations, and amount of perceived risk are different, so making choices for the life you want to lead can be done only by you.

That having been said, I recommend that you follow your instincts and do what is right for you and your family at the time you are making the decision. Ultimately, though, I think back to a class in graduate school that greatly shaped my thinking today. It was a course on Marxist theory that introduced me to the teachings of Marxism and its belief that capitalists (the bourgeoisie) owned and managed the means of production in the world, and that workers (the proletariat) are forced to sell their labor to the bourgeoisie just to survive. The capitalists generate profit by charging more than the value of the workers' production. Capitalists' profits come from maximizing the difference between what they pay the proletariat and what they can sell their production for in the open market. Capitalists are just middlemen who take what the workers produce and resell it for a higher price than they paid the workers to produce it. It seems logical that the savviest of the proletariat would eventually realize this and find a way to eliminate the middlemen by becoming one of them. Armed with years of producing for the bourgeoisie and closely monitoring their activities, a smart worker should be able to duplicate what he sees so that he, too, can maximize his own compensation for the value he creates.

Note: If you are intrigued by these ideas, I suggest reading *Das Kapital* by Karl Marx.

Corporate America

A vibrant middle class is one of the principal advantages of our competitive economic system. A large and growing middle class actually counteracts poverty because it serves as an incentive for individuals to work hard and improve their economic positions in life. It also addresses the concerns of those who feel that the disparity between the rich and the poor in our country is far too great. Given that corporations are becoming wealthier because they are sharing less of the upside (predominantly in the form of earned income and stock options) with their workforces and hoarding the lion's share of the gains for their CEOs and other corporate insiders, perhaps you should consider dedicating a portion of your time to an endeavor that will augment and eventually enhance your income and markedly increase your net worth if you happen to be a 9-to-5 employee without an equity position in your company.

Investing in Apartment Buildings

In the late 1990s, I was working for a technology firm that paid its CEO in excess of $70 million a year. That same company provided generous stock options to its key employees, with many having paper fortunes in excess of $1 million each. When the corporation was sold to a European telephone company, the CEO's entire compensation package (including stock options, salary, and other benefits) amounted to nearly $100 million. He also received a weekly chauffeur service for more than five years, at completely no cost. Shortly after the sale, the employee base was decimated through several rounds of layoffs (which were, for the most part, caused by a rapidly changing economic landscape). If you had been one of those employees who were sustaining themselves only on their earned income and didn't command a CEO-like salary with generous stock options and a golden parachute, you might have found yourself in a rather precarious financial situation. Conversely, had your source of income been more diversified, with a larger portion of it derived from portfolio and passive streams, what happened to your day job might not have mattered as much. Therefore, if you continue to work, you must develop an income diversification plan.

Lesson learned: If you're not a key equity player with a significant stake in your company's future, then you're just another dispensable employee. Don't be taken aback or dismayed if you are downsized and put out of a job one day. You must expect the worst, plan for the unknown, and avoid the financial setbacks that are commonplace in corporate America. Diversifying your income base with portfolio and passive income streams must be an essential part of your financial plan. Your 401(k)s and IRAs just aren't enough to provide financial security over the long term.

In summary, the world we live in is rapidly changing. Being a member of the middle class no longer provides a great deal of economic security, as it did for previous generations. One pink slip, a health crisis, or the loss of a spouse would create a major financial setback for most of us. Diversifying one's sources of income is an essential part of creating a sound financial plan, and investing in apartment buildings should be part of that plan.

Best of luck with your goals, and by all means please let me know how you are progressing.

Please feel free to e-mail me at matt@landlordandinvestor.com with questions and/or feedback about this book.

Chapter Summary

- If you want to succeed in this business or any other, you must never, ever give up.
- The law of attraction states that if your mind is preconditioned to thinking positively about something, you are likely to achieve positive results—and vice versa.
- The class system is unfair and unjust, but the inequalities that prevail must not deter you.
- If you have a day job and it's your only means of generating income, you should consider implementing an income diversification plan. Adding passive and portfolio income is always a prudent path to financial security.

Appendix A

Resources

Web Sites

The following is a list of useful sites:

www.apartments.com: A list of apartments searchable by price, location, and more.

www.bls.gov: Bureau of Labor Statistics.

www.census.gov: U.S. Census Bureau.

www.claritas.com: Demographic data.

www.costar.com: Costar Research.

www.factfinder.census.gov: Data on the physical and financial characteristics of U.S. housing.

www.fanniemae.com: The largest diversified financial company in the world, and the nation's largest source of home mortgage funds.

www.forrent.com: Photos, floor plans, and videos of apartments.

www.landlordandinvestor.com: Join this popular investment club and receive an informative monthly real estate newsletter for free.

www.landlord411.com: A comprehensive source of education, information, and assistance for real estate investors, landlords, and professional property managers.

www.loopnet.com: A site that lets you search thousands of apartment buildings for sale nationwide.

www.mpfresearch.com: MPF Research.

www.mrlandlord.com: A popular Web site where rental owners ask landlording questions and get answers and tips from other landlords.

www.nationalreia.com: National REIA's mission is to develop, support, and promote local real estate investor organizations while serving the interests of the real estate investment industry through networking, education, leadership on legislative issues, and promoting professionalism and standards of excellence in our industry.

www.nmhc.org: National Multi Housing Council.

www.realcapitalanalytics.com: Real Capital Analytics.

www.realtor.com: The official site of the National Association of Realtors.

www.reiclub.com: Real estate investors can browse hundreds of free real estate investing articles to increase their investment education.

www.zillow.com: An online real estate service dedicated to estimating home value.

Appendix B

Quotes

What would life be if we had no courage to attempt anything?

—Vincent van Gogh

➤ ━

An expert is a person who has made all the mistakes that can be made in a very narrow field.

—Niels Bohr (Nobel Prize winner)

➤ ━

Failure is only an opportunity to begin again more intelligently.

—Henry Ford

➤ ━

It takes 20 years to build a reputation and five minutes to ruin it. If you think about that, you'll do things differently.

—Warren Buffett

Appendix B

— —

Persistent people begin their success where others end in failure.

—EDWARD EGGLESTON

— —

My mind is my biggest asset. I expect to win every tournament I play.

—TIGER WOODS

— —

It's hard to beat a person who never gives up.

—BABE RUTH

— —

If you work just for the money, you'll never make it, but if you love what you're doing and you always put the customer first, success will be yours.

—RAY KROC

— —

Always bear in mind that your own resolution to succeed is more important than any other one thing.

—ABRAHAM LINCOLN

— —

Clear your mind of can't.

—SAMUEL JOHNSON

— —

A life is not important except in the impact it has on other lives.

—JACKIE ROBINSON

Quotes

—   —

The fruits of life fall into the hands of those who climb the tree and pick them.

—EARL TUPPER

—   —

Strive for perfection in everything. Take the best that exists and make it better. If it doesn't exist, create it. Accept nothing nearly right or good enough.

—HENRY ROYCE

—   —

Life is like riding a bicycle. To keep your balance, you must keep moving.

—ALBERT EINSTEIN

—   —

Pain is temporary. Quitting lasts forever.

—LANCE ARMSTRONG

—   —

What we think, we become.

—BUDDHA

—   —

I know the price of success: dedication, hard work, and an unremitting devotion to the things you want to see happen.

—FRANK LLOYD WRIGHT

—   —

We must use time as a tool, not as a crutch.

—JOHN F. KENNEDY

—   —

You miss 100 percent of the shots you never take.

—WAYNE GRETZKY

Appendix B

— —

I work hard because I love my work.

—BILL GATES

— —

Victory belongs to the most persevering.

—NAPOLEON BONAPARTE

— —

Always do right. That will gratify some of the people, and astonish the rest.

—MARK TWAIN

— —

I'm a great believer in luck, and I find the harder I work, the more I have of it.

—THOMAS JEFFERSON

— —

To love what you do and feel that it matters—how could anything be more fun?

—KATHARINE GRAHAM

— —

Yesterday is not ours to recover, but tomorrow is ours to win or to lose.

—LYNDON B. JOHNSON

— —

When you combine passion and hard work, then success is always possible.

—ARTE MORENO (OWNER OF THE LOS ANGELES ANGELS)

Quotes

—　—

Well done is better than well said.

—BENJAMIN FRANKLIN

—　—

Never mistake motion for action.

—ERNEST HEMINGWAY

—　—

Press on. Nothing can take the place of persistence.

—CALVIN COOLIDGE

—　—

*Better to do something imperfectly than to do nothing
flawlessly.*

—DR. ROBERT SCHULLER

—　—

*Once you say you're going to settle for second, that's what
happens to you in life.*

—JOHN F. KENNEDY

—　—

*By working faithfully eight hours a day, you may eventually
get to be the boss and work twelve hours a day.*

—ROBERT FROST

Appendix C

Top Multifamily Lenders

AGM Financial Services Inc.
2 North Charles St., Suite 850
Baltimore, MD 21201
(410) 727-2111
www.agmfinancial.com

AmeriSphere Multifamily Finance LLC
One Pacific Place, Suite 130
1125 South 103rd St.
Omaha, NE 68124
(402) 926-3520
www.amerisphere.net

Apollo Equity Partners
600 Superior Ave., Suite 2300
Cleveland, OH 44114
(216) 875-2626
www.apollohousing.com

Apple Bank for Savings
122 East 42nd St.
New York, NY 10168
(212) 224-6456
www.theapplebank.com

Arbor Commercial Mortgage LLC
333 Earle Ovington Blvd., Suite 900
Uniondale, NY 11553
(800) 272-6710
www.thearbornet.com

ARCS Commercial Mortgage
26901 Agoura Rd., Suite 200
Calabasas Hills, CA 91301
(800) 275-2727
www.askarcs.com

Aries Capital
350 West Erie St., Suite 150
Chicago, IL 60610
(312) 642-6164
www.ariescapital.com

Bank of America/Bank of America Securities
100 North Tryon St.
Charlotte, NC 28255
(301) 829-1776
www.bankofamerica.com
commercialrealestate@bankofamerica.com

Beacon Realty Capital Inc.
549 West Randolph St., Suite 700
Chicago, IL 60661
(312) 207-0060
www.beaconrealtycapital.com

Top Multifamily Lenders

Boston Capital Finance
One Boston Pl.
Boston, MA 02108
(617) 624-8900
www.bostoncapital.com

Buchanan Street Partners
620 Newport Center Dr., 8th Floor
Newport Beach, CA 92660
(949) 721-1414
www.buchananst.com

Bulls Capital Partners LLC
8330 Boone Blvd., Suite 800
Vienna, VA 22182
(703) 848-8001
www.bullscapitalpartners.com

Cambridge Realty Capital Cos.
35 East Wacker Dr., 33rd Floor
Chicago, IL 60601
(312) 357-1601
www.cambridgecap.com

Capmark Finance Inc.
200 Witmer Rd.
Horsham, PA 19044
(800) 446-2226
www.gmaccm.com

Capstone Realty Advisors
6241 Riverside Dr.
Columbus, OH 43017
(614) 766-2484
www.capstone-realty.com

CBRE Capital Markets
2800 Post Oak Blvd., Suite 2100
Houston, TX 77056
(713) 787-1900
www.cbre.com/capitalmarkets

Centerline Capital Group
625 Madison Ave., 5th Floor
New York, NY 10022
(212) 317-5700
www.centerline.com

Cohen Financial
Two North LaSalle St., Suite 800
Chicago, IL 60602
(312) 346-5680
www.cohenfinancial.com

Collateral Real Estate Capital LLC
3000 Riverchase Galleria, Suite 1020
Birmingham, AL 35244
(205) 978-1849
www.collateral.com

Column Financial
3414 Peachtree Rd., Suite 400
Atlanta, GA 30326
(404) 239-5000
www.columnfinancial.com

Column Guaranteed LLC
3414 Peachtree Rd., Suite 400
Atlanta, GA 30326
(404) 239-5300
www.columnfinancial.com

Top Multifamily Lenders

The Community Preservation Corp.
28 East 28th St., 9th Floor
New York, NY 10016
(212) 869-5300
www.communityp.com

Corus Bank
3959 North Lincoln Ave.
Chicago, IL 60613
(773) 832-3533
www.corusbank.com

Credit Suisse First Boston LLC
11 Madison Ave.
New York, NY 10016
(212) 325-2000
www.csfb.com

CW Capital
One Charles River Place/63 Kendrick St.
Needham, MA 02494
(781) 707-9300
www.cwcapital.com

David Cronheim Mortgage Co.
205 Main St.
Chatham, NJ 07928
(973) 635-6800
www.cronheimmort.com

Deutsche Bank Commercial Real Estate
60 Wall St.
New York, NY 10005
(212) 250-2500
www.db.com/cre

Appendix C

Dwinn-Shaffer & Co.
30 West Monroe St., Suite 1610
Chicago, IL 60603
(312) 346-9191
www.dwinn.com

Eastdil Secured
11150 Santa Monica Blvd., Suite 1400
Los Angeles, CA 90025
(310) 477-9600
www.securedcapital.com

Eastern Union Commercial
501 Fifth Ave.
New York, NY 10017
(718) 567-8400
www.easternuc.com

EF&A Funding LLC
4746 Eleventh Ave. NE
Seattle, WA 98105
(800) 522-6865
www.efafunding.com

First Sterling Financial Inc.
1155 Northern Blvd
Manhasset, NY 11030
(516) 627-5223
www.firststerling.com

1st Trust Bank for Savings
6525 Quayle Hollow Rd.
Memphis, TN 38120
(901) 259-5444
www.1sttrustbank.com

Top Multifamily Lenders

Fremont Investment & Loan
2425 Olympic Blvd.
Santa Monica, CA 90404
(310) 315-7019
www.1800fremont.com

GE Real Estate
292 Long Ridge Rd.
Stamford, CT 06927
(888) 433-4778
www.gerealestate.com

George Smith Partners
1801 Century Park East, Suite 1910
Los Angeles, CA 90067
(310) 557-8336
www.gspartners.com

Great Lakes Financial Group LP
25200 Chagrin Blvd., Suite 200
Beachwood, OH 44122
(888) 603-3213
www.greatlakesfg.com

Green Park Financial
7501 Wisconsin Ave., Suite 1200
Bethesda, MD 20814
(301) 215-5500
www.greenparkfinancial.com

Greystone Servicing Corp. Inc.
1715 Aaron Brenner Drive, Suite 500
Memphis, TN 38120
(901) 266-0570
www.greyco.com

Appendix C

Hall Financial Group
6801 Gaylord Parkway, Suite 100
Frisco, TX 75034
(972) 377-1100
www.hallfinancial.com

Heitman
191 North Wacker Dr., Suite 2500
Chicago, IL 60606
(312) 855-5700
www.heitman.com

HFF (Holliday Fenoglio Fowler LP)
2000 Post Oak Blvd., Suite 2000
Houston, TX 77056
(713) 852-3500
www.hfflp.com

HomeStreet Capital
2000 Two Union Square, 601 Union St.
Seattle, WA 98101
(800) 999-7909
www.homestreetcapital.com

HSBC Bank USA, NA
452 Fifth Ave., 24th floor
New York, NY 10018
(212) 525-5000
www.us.hsbc.com

Hudson Realty Capital LLC
381 Park Ave. South, Suite 428
New York, NY 10016
(212) 532-3553
www.hudsonrealtycapital.com

Top Multifamily Lenders

iCap Realty Advisors LLC
4576 Research Forest Dr.
The Woodlands, TX 77381
(713) 888-icap
www.icaprealty.com

Inland Mortgage Capital Corp.
1646 North California Blvd.
Walnut Creek, CA 94596
(630) 218-8000
www.inlandmtg.com

Johnson Capital
18101 Von Karman Ave., Suite 1050
Irvine, CA 92612
(949) 660-1999
www.johnsoncapital.com

KeyBank Real Estate Capital
127 Public Square
Cleveland, OH 44114
(888) 539-2221
www.key.com/realestatecapital

LaSalle Bank
135 South LaSalle St., Suite 1225
Chicago, IL 60603
(312) 904-2000
www.lasallebank.com

Laureate Capital LLC
227 West Trade St., Suite 400
Charlotte, NC 28202
(704) 379-6910
www.laureatecapital.com

Appendix C

LMI Capital Inc.
1776 Woodstead Ct., Suite 208
The Woodlands, TX 77380
(281) 363-4920
www.lmicapital.com

Love Funding Corp.
212 South Central, Suite 301
St. Louis, MO 63105
(314) 512-7950
www.lovefunding.com

Madison Capital Group
1 SE Third Ave., Suite 3120
Miami, FL 33131
(305) 375-9110
www.madisoncapitalgroup.com

M&T Bank Corp.
1 M&T Plaza
Buffalo, NY 14203
(716) 842-5445
www.mandtbank.com

Meecorp Capital Markets LLC
2115 Linwood Ave.
Fort Lee, NJ 07024
(201) 944-9330
www.meecorp.com

Mercury Capital
317 Madison Ave.
New York, NY 10017
(212) 661-8700
www.mercurycapital.com

Top Multifamily Lenders

Meridian Capital Group
1 Battery Park Plaza
New York, NY 10004
(212) 972-3600
www.meridiancapital.com

Merrill Lynch & Co.
4 World Financial Center
New York, NY 10080
(212) 449-3450
www.ml.com

Mezz Cap
51 JFK Pkwy., 4th Floor
Short Hills, NJ 07078
(973) 467-6000
www.mezzcapfinance.com

MMA Financial
621 East Pratt St.
Baltimore, MD 21202
(800) 237-9946
www.mmafin.com

Morgan Stanley
1585 Broadway
New York, NY 10036
(212) 761-4000
www.morganstanley.com/realestate/index.html

Mountain Funding LLC
11600 North Community House Rd.
Charlotte, NC 28277
(704) 540-7400
www.mountainfunding.com

NorthMarq Capital Inc.
3500 American Blvd. West
Bloomington, MN 55431
(952) 356-0100
www.northmarq.com

Northwestern Mutual
720 East Wisconsin Ave.
Milwaukee, WI 53202
(414) 271-1444
www.northwesternmutualinvestments.com

The Park Avenue Bank
460 Park Ave.
New York, NY 10022
(212) 755-4600
www.parkavenuebank.com

PNC Multifamily Capital
249 Fifth Ave.
Pittsburgh, PA 15243
(800) 481-4874
www.pncrealestatefinance.com

P/R Mortgage & Investment Corp.
11711 North Meridian St., Suite 528
Carmel, IN 46032
(317) 569-7420
www.prmic.com

Primary Capital Advisors
2060 Mt. Paran Rd., Suite 101
Atlanta, GA 30327
(404) 365-9300
www.primarycapital.com

Top Multifamily Lenders

Principal Real Estate Investors
801 Grand Ave.
Des Moines, IA 50392
(800) 533-1390
www.principalglobal.com

Prudential Mortgage Capital Co.
100 Mulberry St., GC4, 8th Floor
Newark, NJ 07102
(888) 263-6800
www.prudential.com/mortgagecapital

Q10 Capital LLC
111 East Broadway, Suite 1250
Salt Lake City, UT 84111
(801) 323-1088
www.q10capital.com

Red Capital Group
2 Miranova Place, 12th Floor
Columbus, OH 43215
(800) 837-5100
www.redcapitalgroup.com

Regional Capital Group
701 Route 70 East
Marlton, NJ 08053
(856) 983-4800
www.regionalcapital.com

Sierra Capital Partners Inc.
18500 Von Karman Ave., Suite 515
Irvine, CA 92612
(949) 428-8888
www.sierracp.com

Appendix C

Sonnenblick-Goldman Co.
712 Fifth Ave.
New York, NY 10019
(212) 841-9200
www.sonngold.com

Sterling Commercial Capital
60 Katona Dr., Suite 22
Fairfield, CT 06824
(203) 366-0320
www.sterlingcommercialcapital.com

Strategic Alliance Mortgage LLC
95 Merrick Way, Suite 360
Coral Gables, FL 33134
(305) 447-7820
www.samalliance.com

SunAmerica Affordable Housing Partners Inc.
1999 Avenue of the Stars
Century City, CA 90067
(310) 772-6000
www.saahp.com

TIAA-CREF
730 Third Ave., 4th floor
New York, NY 10017
(800) 542-2252
www.tiaacref.org

Transwestern Commercial Services
1900 West Loop South, Suite 1300
Houston, TX 77027
(713) 270-7700
www.transwestern.net

Top Multifamily Lenders

Tremont Realty Capital
800 Boylston St., Suite 401
Boston, MA 02199
(617) 867-0700
www.tremontcapital.com

Trump Mortgage LLC
40 Wall St., 25th Floor
New York, NY 10005
(888) 798-7867
www.trumpmortgage.com

Union Capital Investments LLC
3490 Piedmont Rd. NE, Suite 1010
Atlanta, GA 30305
(404) 812-4800
www.ucillc.com

ValueXpress LLC
200 East 42nd St., 9th Floor
New York, NY 10017
(800) 650-2627
www.valuexpress.com

Wachovia Multifamily Capital
6 East 43rd St, 26th Floor
New York, NY 10017
(212) 250-4200
www.apflending.com
Source of capital: Fannie Mae, Freddie Mac

Wachovia Securities
301 South College St.
Charlotte, NC 28202
(704) 383-6315
www.wachovia.com

Appendix C

Washington Mutual
1301 Second Ave.
Seattle, WA 98101
(877) 926-8273
www.wamu.com

Wells Fargo Multifamily Capital
2010 Corporate Ridge, Suite 1000
McLean, VA 22102
(877) 734-5592
www.wellsfargo.com/wfcm

Wextrust Capital
318 West Adams, Suite 500
Chicago, IL 60606
(312) 881-6000
www.wextrust.com

Index

Index

Index

Index

Index

in overall class structure, 8–9
poverty, 12–13
Moran & Co., 66
Mortgage Bankers Association, 19
Mortgage lenders, 70–72
"Mortgage meltdown: vulture investors"
(CNN), 74
MRI management software, 158
MSPA (Mystery Shopping Providers Association), 148
Multifamily brokerage firms listing, 64–66
Multifamily financing (*See* Financing)
Multifamily residential properties, 25–38
defined, 26
five or more units, 33–38
two to four units, 25–31
Mystery Shopping Providers Association
(MSPA), 148

National Association of Realtors (NAR), 166
National conferences, 68
National Fair Housing Alliance, 155
National Multi Housing Council (NMHC),
41, 68
National Review, 11
Negotiating prices, 84–85
Net operating income (NOI), increasing,
55–61, 116
New home start trends, 165
New Orleans, 185–186
New York Times, 11, 13, 17, 19, 21, 184
Newsletter ads, 73
Newspaper ads and listings, 73–74, 150
NMHC (National Multi Housing Council),
41, 68
NOI (net operating income), increasing,
55–61, 116
Non-owner-occupied units, 19, 29
Nonrecourse debt, 35

Obama, Barack and Michelle, 11
Office buildings, 174–177
Off-site property management, 147–148
O'Neal, Stan, 12–13
Online research, 68–69, 109–110
On-site management software, 158
On-site property management, 111–112,
158
Open house, 151
Operating expenses, 36, 79

Owner involvement, 157–158
Owner-occupant, 29

Passive income, 6–7
Patience, importance of, 53–55
PBGC (Pension Benefit Guaranty Corp.), 13
PCA (property condition assessment) report,
98–99
Pension Benefit Guaranty Corp. (PBGC), 13
Pension plans, 13–14
Personal network resources, 69–70
Pipeline report, 51–52
Police call-out records, 112
Population trends, 160–161, 165
Portable On Demand Storage (PODS), 166
Portfolio income, 7
Positive cash flow properties, compared with
speculation properties, 60–61
Postal carrier, 111
Poverty and social class, 12–13
Prepayment penalties, 137
Price negotiations, 84–85
Pro forma statements, 79–82
Properties:
categories from mortgage lenders, 70–72
commercial, 174–177
in default, 70, 86–87
discounted, 82–84
distressed, 70
financing, 135
finding undervalued, 68–75
institutional-sized, 37
positive cash flow, 60–61
speculation, 60–61
Property condition assessment (PCA) report,
98–99
Property data, 97–98
Property inspection, 98–102
Property location grades, 46
Property management, 139–162
company:
vs. establishing own team, 144–146
vs. property manager, 142–144
comparative market analysis (CMA),
148–149
compensating property manager, 146–147
discrimination, 154–155
finding new tenants, 149–151
landlord vs. investor, 141–142
"large" multifamily properties, 34, 36

219

Index

Index

About the Author

 Matthew Martinez is an accomplished investor of value-add multifamily properties, spokesperson for Intuit's rental property management software, an AOL money/real estate coach, founder of one of the country's largest real estate investment groups, and a bestselling author of real estate investment books. He has been featured in the *Wall Street Journal, Money Magazine,* the *Daily Business Review,* CNBC, and Reuters. CNN called him a "tycoon in the making!"

Please visit Matthew at: www.matthewamartinez.com

Real Estate Scholarship

The Matthew A. Martinez Real Estate Scholarship was established to promote the study of real estate. This fund awards scholarships to students studying real estate at the undergraduate and graduate levels.

Eligibility criteria: To be eligible, the applicant must be an undergraduate or graduate student currently enrolled full-time at an accredited four-year college or university with a declared major or minor in real estate.

Amount: A portion of the royalties from the sale of this book will be dedicated to this scholarship program.

Additional information: To learn more about the Matthew A. Martinez Real Estate Scholarship or to obtain an application, please visit the following Web site:

http://matthewamartinez.com/Scholarship.html.

Or e-mail me at matt@landlordandinvestor.com.

Thank you to all of the sponsors who contributed to the
Matthew A. Martinez Real Estate Scholarship:

Parents Have To Worry About A Lot Of Things.

Where Their Children Are Going To Sleep

Should Not Have To Be One of Them.

Travelers Aid Family Services

is the goal of Travelers Aid Family Services to end homelessness in Boston

One Family at a Time

Within our *Continuum of Care* is the *TAFS Homes* program, which purchases and renovates small multi-family residences of 3 to 6 units en selects as tenants homeless families living in shelters or families at-isk of becoming homeless. Travelers Aid Family Services performs the perty maintenance and agency social workers provide professional case management to all tenants to ensure access to mainstream services, workforce development skills and job placement.

ounded in 1920, Travelers Aid Family Services is one of the leading service agencies in Boston. To help accomplish our mission, we administer a variety of programs, which range from prevention of homelessness and emergency shelter for families, to transitional elter and permanent affordable housing. Over the last year, Travelers Aid Family Services provided support for over 700 families through these programs.

f you would like to learn more about Travelers Aid Family Services or make a donation, please visit

www.tafsboston.org or call 617-542-7286

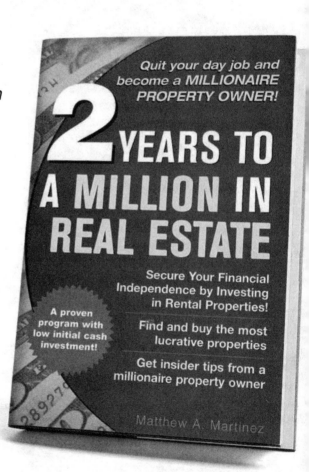